DESIGNED DESTINATIONS

Every Entrepreneur's Guide
to a Successful Business
Sale or Transfer

LAWRENCE J. GANIM

COPYRIGHT

First published in 2017 by Lawrence J. Ganim. ©Copyright Lawrence J. Ganim.

All rights reserved. No part of this publication may be reproduced, stored in or introduced into a retrieval system, or transmitted in any form, or by any means (electronic, mechanical, photocopying, recording or otherwise,) without the prior written permission of the publisher. This book is sold on the condition that it shall not, by any way of trade or otherwise, be lent, resold, hired out, or otherwise circulated, without the publisher's prior consent, in any form.

Disclaimer

This book is not intended to provide personalized legal, financial, or investment advice. The author disclaims any liability, loss or risk which is incurred as a consequence, directly or indirectly, of the use and application of any contents of this work. Lawrence J. Ganim does not offer tax or legal advice. Any decisions whether to implement any ideas shared in this book should be made by the individual in consultation with professional financial, tax and legal counsel.

www.Designed-Destinations.com

ISBN 13: 978-1976214219
ISBN-10: 1976214211

DEDICATION

I would like to dedicate this book to all those I have had the privilege to help and learn from over the past 36 years: My family, clients and friends.

Acknowledgments

I would like to acknowledge my father and mother, John and Mary Ganim, who shared with me the many values I have to this day. My father taught me the true value of work and honesty, and my mother's boundless love, friendship and belief in me throughout my life is a foundation I am eternally grateful for.

For my wife, Diane, who has always trusted in my judgment and supported me throughout our journey walking through life together, never asking why, only telling me to go for it; I believe in you.

To my business partner, Valerie, who has always been there to support and encourage me on all levels, trusting in my dreams and desires and supporting me all the way. It was Valerie who pushed me to fulfill my dream of writing a book and stop dreaming and start doing.

Last, but surely not least, my four amazing children who I have the pleasure and privilege of sharing this life with. Robert, Christopher, Lauren, and Jessica. I am so proud of the men and women they have grown into and I give thanks every day for these amazing gifts that are my children!

CONTENTS

PREFACE	ix
A failure to plan…	xi
Where I come in	xii
PART ONE: A FUTURE BY CHANCE OR A FUTURE BY DESIGN	1
CHAPTER 1: THE DEVIL TAKES THE HINDMOST	3
Surprising Attitudes	6
House Rules	8
CHAPTER 2: BEWARE THE ENEMY WITHIN	11
How Your *Strengths* Quickly Turn to *Liabilities*	13
CHAPTER 3: THE 'WORK TRAP'	17
Reason #1: The Squeaky Wheel Gets the Grease	18
Reason #2: A Little Knowledge Is a Dangerous Thing	23
Reason #3: Business Owners Can't Buy Into the Vocabulary	26
CHAPTER 4: KNOW YOUR DESTINATION	31
You Will Need a TEAM	33
Pulling It Together	35
Are You Ready?	41
PART TWO: 7 KEY STEPS TO A SOUND OCP	43
CHAPTER 5: CEMENT YOUR FUTURE VISION	47
Get ready for 'Gap Shock'	50
What Is GAP Shock and Where It Can Impact You	54

CHAPTER 6: THE SIZE OF THE POT	59
Why A Personal Hedge (Ph) Is Important	62
How you can do it	66
CHAPTER 7: TURNING YOUR BUSINESS INTO A BUTTERFLY	69
Leadership Resources	70
Rewarding/Retaining Key personnel	72
Bonus Plans	75
Human Resources Management	76
Financial and Legal Management	79
Customer and Product Management	82
Operating Systems and Technology	86
Owner Management	87
CHAPTER 8: THE EMPTY CHAIR	91
Your Business Will	92
What Is a Purchase Put Option (PPO)?	100
CHAPTER 9: YOUR PERSONAL HEDGE	109
CHAPTER 10: THE INTERSECTION: CHOOSING YOUR INSIDE/OUTSIDE SALE OPTION	115
Outsider Sale Planning	119
CHAPTER 11: THE HARVEST – REAPING EVERYTHING YOUR EFFORTS HAVE ACHIEVED	125
Sale to Insiders	128
Sale to Outsiders	129
It's All One Pie So Handle It Accordingly	131
Mesh your Plans	134
CONCLUSION: A FUTURE BY CHANCE OR A FUTURE BY DESIGN?	137
CHAPTER 12: FINAL EXAM	139
ABOUT THE AUTHOR	143

Preface

Dreams versus dreams realized — the difference is what I consider to be inspired, conscious action.

My business and yours started out on some level as a dream or a means to fulfill a dream. The actions we took and continue to take are due to what I call inspired, conscious action. Inspired, conscious action is action inspired and driven by a solid vision of the outcomes we seek. No clear vision, no inspired conscious actions are possible. I think we all have seen that time and again as we managed our ventures.

Well, an essential part of your business journey lies somewhere down the road — it's just a matter of time. It involves the day when you seek to turn your business into cash, pass the baton, ensure the legacy created by your dreams and inspired actions, and protect the impact that all has on those we all serve on some level, including ourselves, our family, our employees, our community, and those who choose to utilize our products and/or services.

I'm here to tell you that this ultimate destination along your business journey does not turn out well by means of good luck or happy accidents, or fortuitous circumstance. In my experience, this too only results from design.

Every entrepreneur, regardless of what stage we are at in our business and career, has the same fears and concerns and desires. We all have those nights when we wake up in the middle of the night fearing an outcome that may or may not be likely. We all have those days, sometimes weeks, sometimes months when we feel we could conquer the world and nothing will ever stop us. And we all have those times where we wonder how we are going to make payroll the next month, or meet the obligations we have personally and for our business.

We are all very different, yet I believe we are all cut from the same cloth.

Many business owners dream about the day they successfully sell or transition their business and retire. What business owner doesn't want that?

You will reach that destination in one of two ways — by conscious design or by unconscious design. Conscious design can help you realize the legacy you envision: Lifestyle security, family harmony, social responsibility. Unconscious design rarely reaches a destination you envision and can leave you with a legacy you fear. Fear is a naysayer; we create outcomes based on fear or based upon a clear vision of what we desire.

I dreamed of writing this book years ago, but never acted. I never took action because I wasn't really sure how to do it and how to make it a reality. I never took the next steps until some very wise words spoken by my then 15-year-old daughter, Jessica, helped to inspire me: "You can never complete an essay if you don't start the first sentence"!

So, let's take a look at what it might take to start our first sentence so to speak of your ownership conversion plan (OCP) and some of the benefits of such a plan.

PREFACE

A failure to plan…

A consciously designed ownership conversion plan (OCP) ensures that you, the owner/founder, are in full control of a realistic and timely approach to passing on your business and leaving it in a manner and at a time that you choose, your Designed Destinations.

With it, you have sufficient assets outside of your business to give you the lifestyle you desire, and your business asset becomes the frosting on the cake.

Your OCP ensures that your business and those who rely on your business continue uninterrupted for potentially generations. Because you have this plan in place, it helps you to make what I call inspired business decisions to ensure that your business is maximized on all levels and remains profitable and viable under multiple conditions and can effectively weather the many storms that are part of business life.

An inspired decision is one made with you being fully aware of the outcomes you seek on all levels and how this decision will impact the vision you now have in place due to your OCP. You know what you're doing and why; it empowers more effective decisions on a daily, weekly and yearly basis guided by the vision you have created for the future of your business. You have a clear vision of where you are headed and why. Your OCP functions as your roadmap helping to guide the creation and management of your strategic planning and the ongoing decision process that is part of that.

An unconscious design means you are at the mercy of your business and in effect flying by the seat of your pants and betting that it will all work out somehow. Your business succession or sale is up to whatever the situation is when that time comes. Your ability to retire is very reliant on what you might get out of the business upon sale, and your retirement lifestyle is very dependent on that number, whatever it might be.

You are not in the drivers' seat when and if you end up negotiating the sale or transfer of your business to those inside or outside of your business. Decisions are based on the crisis of the moment. The associated tax bills connected with any transfer or sale of your business will likely be much higher than they need be. You find yourself making 11th-hour decisions on methods and terms. You and your family will likely end up with much less in your pocket at the end of this process.

Where I come in

I wanted to write this book to help create clarity for the majority of business owners who are really unsure of how to approach this planning and therefore don't do it at all. Or maybe they do so in a haphazard way that does not lead them to the position that a solid OCP can help create for them.

Imagine this, an investment of the equivalent of ONE DAY of your time can be the difference of potentially millions of dollars in your pocket and a future that is

Preface

clear and understandable by all involved. Invest ONE DAY now and avoid years of uncertainty!

You will experience almost immediate benefits by utilizing a solid OCP planning process. Over the years, we have evolved a 7 step process to creating and executing a solid OCP plan. I have learned from many sources, including clients, advisors and others in this planning space. To say all of what I will share with you is totally original would be an untruth. I am a student for life and always learning from multiple sources and always open to new ideas and methods of managing an effective OCP in all of its forms.

My experience comes from working for more than 30 years with successful entrepreneurs, as well as experiencing my own family's challenges with this reality along with my own personal experience as a business owner. In all cases, owners eventually face the concerns and opportunities that can be addressed by a effectively created and executed OCP and the clarity it can provide for ongoing decisions associated with managing this very significant yet personal asset that we call our business. I have seen the outcomes and benefits of poor decisions as well as the outcomes and benefits of inspired decisions. The difference is monumental.

You and I will begin a journey in the following chapters designed to help inspire you to make a decision to create YOUR designed destinations. Let's get started on our journey and start our first sentence!

Part One

A Future by Chance or a Future by Design

Chapter 1

The Devil Takes the Hindmost

How much of your business success can you attribute to good luck, to happy accidents, or fortuitous coincidence?

All entrepreneurs enjoy positive results from being in the right place at the right time, but few would be willing to attribute success to those events. And few would assign lady luck a prominent role in their business plan. They know that their businesses grew because they planned it that way. And when the plan got stuck, they stepped back and adjusted it.

Growing a business requires tremendous attention, emotion and will — and some luck doesn't hurt. But it always starts, and continues, and prospers with a plan. So exactly why is it that so many business owners don't have the vision to make sure it also **ends** with a plan?

If you take a long hard look at the state of most small- to medium-sized businesses today, that basic planning premise is largely absent when it comes to the inevitable exiting or selling of the operation. Consider:

- At any given time, 40 percent of U.S. businesses are facing the transfer of ownership issue.

- An estimated 63 percent of business owners lack a written strategic plan for running their business.[1]

- Even those who are not looking to exit are concerned about the future and preserving their options.[2]

- From January 2011 to December 2020 10,000 baby boomers are projected to turn 65 every day.[3]

- Over 75 percent of baby-boomer business owners have no exit plan or any idea how to handle what will be the biggest financial decision.[4]

- 64 percent of owners say that retirement and succession planning are their most pressing concerns, yet over 80 percent of firms have no succession plan.[5]

Those statistics and more lead me to tell you that, when it comes to sale and succession planning, most closely held businesses are exposed to the risk equivalent to a single spin of the roulette wheel in a casino.

---

1 The Exit Planning Process, A Financial Services Group, 2010. Down Market Presents Exit Strategy Opportunities For Business Owners, National Underwriter, 02 Apr 2011
2 Entrepreneur, Sell Your Company With Savvy, 4/2/10.
3 Boom or Bust…How the baby boomer Agewave affects you?, Business Broker Blog, 29 Mar 2011
4 Ibid.
5 The Exit Planning Process, A Financial Services Group, 2010.

A second set of statistics should convince you that such a spin of the wheel with your most valuable asset is not likely to turn out well. Consider:

- While over 50 percent of owners would like to exit or sell their business, only 1 percent successfully do so each year. [6]

- Around 30 percent of transfer failures become business closures. [7]

- Only 30 percent of businesses survive to the 2nd generation of leadership. [8]

- An average of only 10 percent are successful in the 3rd generation. [9]

- Poor planning has left 96 percent of small business owners unable to exit their business on their own schedule. [10] Their time is consumed by running the business, which leaves little time left to focus on their exit strategy. [11]

- What many owners believe will be a quick journey to retirement ends up requiring two to three years

---

6   Entrepreneur, Sell Your Company With Savvy, 4/2/10.
7   Passing Your Business on to the Next Generation: Is It Best for Your Family?, Business Know How, 2011. Passing the baton – encouraging successful business transfers: Evidence and key stakeholder opinion, Small Business Service – Durham University Business School, undated.
8   Passing Your Business on to the Next Generation: Is It Best for Your Family?, Business Know How, 2011. Passing the baton – encouraging successful business
9   Entrepreneur, Sell Your Company With Savvy, 4/2/10.
10 Your Business: Will It Have A Happy Ending?, Brader Green, 29 Mar 2011. Don't Delay – Begin to Plan Now, Talent C, 4 Mar 2011. Financial Planning, 1 Oct 2010. Exit strategy
11 The Exit Planning Process, A Financial Services Group, 2010. Down Market Presents Exit Strategy Opportunities For Business Owners, National Underwriter, 02 Apr 2011.

of planning, process adjustments, and grooming of a successor.[12]

- The primary cause for failure is lack of planning according to the Small Business Administration.
- Owners who have an effective plan have a 106 percent increase in profit over those who have no succession plan.[13]

Surprising Attitudes

I have had the privilege of working with extremely successful business owners for more than three decades. However, early in my financial advisor career, it was easy to assume that these business owners, who were worth tens and hundreds of millions of dollars, were "all set." They told me they were covered, and I respected their confidence.

But all of that changed after deeper analysis. I learned that virtually nothing was taken care of for most. Here are some firsthand experiences to consider.

One client described how a son-in-law who was a leading law professor at an Ivy League university had advised him that all his ducks were in a row. But with closer examination, it became apparent that even basic planning had not been implemented. How about only having a simple will for an estate worth more than fifty million dollars!

---

12 Your Business: Will It Have A Happy Ending?, Brader Green, 29 Mar 2011. Don't Delay – Begin to Plan Now, Talent C, 4 Mar 2011. Financial Planning, 1 Oct 2010. Exit strategy.

13 Ibid.

On another occasion, I was introduced to a company with more than a dozen owners, all offspring of the three brothers who were the original owners. The brothers had no funded agreements in place to transfer their ownership at death, and had no estate planning to protect the value of the business. The three founders died over a relatively short period, and ownership was divided equally among the next generation.

Of course, by this time, there was no serious interest among the heirs to actually work in the business. On the other hand, they were seriously interested in the distributions from the company they were to receive. Of course, the distributions meant none of the profits could be reinvested in the business, so growth slowed and eventually the management team running the company lost their motivation and left. Worse, the numerous heirs hired separate attorneys and accountants to look out for each of their individual needs, making decision-making impossible. There was too little planning, begun way too late to save this company. The company ended up being liquidated with employees out of work and heirs out of money.

I grew up in a family business with a firsthand understanding of the benefits and the pitfalls of business ownership. Our business never had a plan, never had answers for questions about future direction, never realized how much unnecessary money was going down the tax rat hole.

My father was a product of the Great Depression who managed to grow a vegetable peddler cart into a successful nursery business and a large net worth. His early history taught him to save money, but planning — not so much. I nagged him for years until, finally, he understood how important planning would be to his three sons. We met and I conceptually designed a very effective plan to protect the business value and minimize estate taxes. The next week he died, before any elements of the plan could be implemented.

Of course, the IRS cleaned our clocks. Still, we managed to save the business, which my oldest brother continues to manage as my father desired. But no actual design for the future was put in place despite that experience. Eventually, due completely to the negative impact of having no effective Ownership Conversion Plan, conflicts rose among us, and our family relationships remain contentious even today.

House Rules

In roulette, the table odds are set up so that the house (the casino) wins more than 90 percent of the time when the ball begins to roll. Each spin of the wheel offers you less than a 10 percent chance of winning. You can devise different strategies for placing bets, but none will put you ahead of the odds.

The same is true for your business. If you don't have a plan in place for succession or sale, you leave the future of your business purely to chance. The statistics, supported by my experience with business owners over the past three decades, show that selling your business to outsiders, insiders, or family offers about the same odds of winning.

Despite all these statistics and examples, understand that you can take control of the Ownership Conversion choices, and not leave the outcome to chance.

You can control your priorities and focus your energy on the solutions to critical concerns.

You can control the value of your company and the method of monetizing that value.

You can control the tax consequences.

You can control your responses to the impact of change in your company, in your marketplace, and in the financial and economic environments.

In the next chapter, I'll begin to show you how. You CAN design your destination.

Takeaways

- Most small- or medium-sized businesses don't have an ownership conversion plan in place, and place their future at risk.
- The dismal odds against businesses outliving their founders shouldn't deter you from taking action.
- All it takes to beat the odds is discovering the right destination for your business and learning how to make the right design decisions to reach it.

Chapter 2

Beware the Enemy Within

I HAVE been advising business owners for over three decades. When you spend that amount of time with entrepreneurs, you recognize and appreciate both the qualities and the kinship they share.

This experience also has taught me about the complexities and contradictions that make business owners so intriguing and enjoyable as clients. I believe three of these qualities have a primary impact on the success of all Ownership Conversion and monetization strategies. Let's start by analyzing these three entrepreneurial qualities:

- **Autonomy**: Independent and free to control our futures.
- **Self-confidence**: Belief in ourselves and what we are capable of doing.
- **Conscientiousness**: Always having a backup plan of action to reach an outcome.

Whenever I meet with business owners who are approaching the most important decisions about the future of their companies, I ask them the question below.

If you were at the casino playing the roulette wheel, would you risk your whole business on the single turn of that wheel?

The answer I get to that question from business owners is universally, *NO!*

That *NO* is your Autonomy talking.

You fight to gain control over every aspect of your business. That means you don't need anyone else, and you don't depend on luck. And you're right.

Sure, you have managers and advisors who can sweat the operational stuff, the technical stuff, the legal and financial stuff. You respect and value their expertise and experience. But the reality is, for the final say, they come to you.

That *NO* also is your Self-confidence talking.

You trust your instincts, your intuition, your perception, your intellect. When challenges back you into a corner, you know that somehow, some way you will find a solution. Okay, some nights you go to bed full of doubt, but by the time dawn lights the sky, you see the answer you need.

If you trust yourself, it's never a gamble. You see the goal. You start down the path. You navigate the obstacles and detours. You reach the goal. Simple and reliable.

And last, that *NO* is your Conscientiousness talking.

You may appear to be overly enthusiastic and chronically impatient, but even when your emotions amp up, your mind is coolly calculating the process from start to finish. Risk-taker? Maybe, but you don't work without a net.

Risk tolerance comes from having Plan A in place and Plan B waiting in the background. Risk your business on one spin of the wheel? You would never purposely put yourself in that position.

Yet, time and again, when business owners prepare to convert their business into their legacy, these three qualities which contributed to their success also end up to have worked against them.

How Your *Strengths* Quickly Turn to *Liabilities*

The flip side of Autonomy, Self-confidence, and Conscientiousness leads business owners to defer and delay preparing their companies for Ownership Conversion. You invest all your time and energy working *in* the business and ignore working *on* the business.

Plus, you may take these same qualities and think that, if you apply them to selling your business you will be as successful as you were running our business. Not the case.

Here's how it can happen to you.

The ultimate benchmark of your company's success is its longevity. The ultimate family goals are to achieve your future workstyle/lifestyle ideal, and create financial security for your life and family over generations. Your business is the asset that will achieve that future, but you will have to monetize that asset and leave the longevity to someone else.

Young, first-time entrepreneurs have high expectations to turn their innovative ideas into a public offering within months. But business owners with mature businesses don't typically begin contemplating their end game until they reach their fifties. For mature businesses and business owners, there are three different scenarios to choose from.

- Sell to an outside buyer.
- Engage with inside buyers.
- Transfer among family members.

There is a fourth scenario, but no business owner I have worked with wants any part of it.

- Liquidate the company.

When I say business owners get *serious* about Ownership Conversion by age fifty, I don't necessarily mean *realistic*.

Because they love what they do, they imagine that in ten or fifteen years they will slow down, letting go of the day-to-day grind to concentrate on vision and directions for future growth—part time CEO at full pay.

That can be realistic, but only if you are willing to start today. If you wait, you won't make the necessary decisions and take the needed actions until the window of opportunity is closing.

Merger &Acquisition cycles might not support your sale goals. Co-owners may decide it's too late to take full ownership and control. Or your own management team might not gel effectively enough to become potential owners. Family members or protégés could regret they agreed to become your clones.

So, the ten-to-fifteen years you set as your horizon shortens to five and you still don't have an ownership transfer plan. Five turns into a rolling five until your horizon turns to sunset and you are staring at one spin of the Ownership Conversion roulette wheel. What made it happen?

- Your Autonomy asset became inflexibility.
- Your Self-confidence became over-confidence.
- Your conscientiousness never showed up for Ownership Conversion planning.

Takeaways

- Don't wait too long to get serious about designing your company's destination.
- Get more than serious; get realistic.
- Put the same skills that helped you stay in control and manage your risk while growing your business to work on designing your business destination.

Chapter 3

The 'Work Trap'

"The Journey of 1000 miles begins with a single step"
—Chinese Proverb

Why do so many business owners fail to engage in Ownership Conversion planning? Because most continue to work *in* the business and fail to step back and work *on* the business.

Here's your dilemma. When you look at your business and personal finances, you feel you are doing quite well by the standards of most owners. But you are not sure how much income you will need when you decide to slow down or move on from your business. So, you don't know if — or how — your business will provide sufficient retirement income for your lifestyle and legacy goals.

As long as you have been in business, you have faced obstacles, devised plans, and solved problems. Yet this one may turn out to be your biggest dilemma and you don't have a plan. You're not alone. It's a dilemma that

100 percent of the successful entrepreneurs have faced. Here are some reasons why business owners continually wrestle with this dilemma without resolving it.

Reason #1: The Squeaky Wheel Gets the Grease

You are already woken up every night by business decisions that need to be made, and today's problem always seems to need to come first. And those decision "bucks" always ends up on your desk.

What's the best way to increase profitability?

- Increase sales.
- Reduce expenses.
- Improve financial management.
- Invest in efficient systems.

How can we get more from our executive team?

- Commit to more competitive compensation.
- Add perks and benefits.
- Expand performance-based incentives.
- Offer ownership opportunities.

How can we manage risks and liabilities more effectively?

- Shift our risks with broader coverage.
- Reduce our expense by retaining risks.
- Verify our bulletproof contracts.
- Audit our HR and environmental compliance.

How can we strengthen our marketing results?

- Give our brand and value proposition a makeover.
- Increase service to improve customer loyalty.
- Expand market share with product diversity.
- Capture new markets with product innovation.

The real list could go on for pages, and you are the one with the responsibility for making all these decisions. There's no room for problems that are 5-10 years away.

An Evolving Vision

I have a 55-year-old client who created and grew an enterprise to the point where he had more than 90 employees and was generating more than $15 million in revenue per year, while passing $2.5 million in taxable income to the owner and his family.

Yet, he had liquid savings of only $250,000, because most of his after-tax funds went to maintaining his lifestyle. A brilliant business owner, but not so brilliant when it came to personal wealth management.

Having no clear idea of what he would do with his business, or how much income he would need come retirement, and having difficulty saving money, he felt his only way out was to sell his business. But to whom, for how much, and would it be enough to support the lifestyle he and his spouse had grown accustomed to?

I convinced him to step back and consider all the elements that he needed to control. We created a retirement plan option that will allow him and his spouse to save close to $700,000 per year while impacting his spending pattern by about half as much as what he was currently paying in taxes. We agreed upon a future income objective and, after looking at all the options, decided to structure his business so it can and will run with or without him.

Fast forward six years and his savings have grown to more than $6 million and will continue to swell. We are now waiting for the next generation to develop into his Ownership Conversion Plan, with a fallback position of an outside sale. He has put, and is consciously placing, key people in positions and systems in place to enable the business to continue to flourish with or without my client engaged on a daily basis while generation II is being groomed for their role in the business.

Either way, he has established control, which allows him and his spouse to know they will be able to support their future lifestyle. He still has business decisions that may wake him up at night, but what will happen when it comes time for him to sell his business is not one of them.

Sure, you can't let problems fester. But a new today's problem will be waiting for you tomorrow.

Adjust to Change

About ten years ago, I worked with a company to develop an Ownership Conversion Plan for the founder, his daughter and her husband, who were both active in the company. Midway through the plan design, the Great Recession brought cash flow problems. Their capacity for longer-term planning waned, and rational concerns about the future were overwhelmed by emotional concerns about the present.

At the time, the world economy was under extreme duress, which for sophisticated investors usually is a good time to calm down and discover opportunities that would not have occurred in a safer environment. But that kind of intrepid reaction is tough for business owners.

My clients weathered the setbacks in the business due to the economic realities without any drastic changes to the company or the family, but they realized their reaction had unnecessarily put the company at risk. The interruption of the conversion planning could have been disastrous if the founder suffered a disabling health episode or worse. There was no clear vision of how the business would be settled in the event of my client not being able to be fully engaged. The client didn't have an alternative source of income other than the business, the estate and business documents would have placed the active daughter in the business in direct opposition with the siblings outside of the business. They asked me to plug back in, and now the stock has been transferred, which allowed me to effectively integrate business planning with estate planning. The client is now fully retired from the business and with the other children treated fairly with other assets.

Others have not been so fortunate.

I worked with a business that had been purchased from the founder by three employees. They now wanted to sell to an outsider based on the company's growth under their ownership.

My analysis told me their first priority should be what I call a Personal Hedge (PH). A PH involves building assets outside the business to bring balance and diversity to their personal wealth management strategies. Two of the owners followed through, but the third deferred, leaving his financial house constructed out of straw.

In the meantime, I designed an Ownership Conversion Plan with the destination of either an outside buyer or an inside sale to a new layer of internal management eager to build their own house of bricks. But this time, all three delayed implementation of several critical components of the plan and it failed to solidify. The Ownership Conversion Plan became a house built of sticks. They did not act aggressively enough in the funding of the PH plans that were created for them, thereby continuing their very high dependency on the business asset value for future financial security.

In a very short time, the market for their services dramatically changed due to competition and pricing pressures brought on by technology and the economy. Companies they served decided to bring in-house the services my clients provided, leaving them out in the cold — with the wolf. They were forced to reduce their hundred employees, and eventually were left with only three.

Planning for an internal sale became superfluous. Any opportunity for an external sale was lost. The one victory was that the two owners who adopted a Personal Hedge were saved.

So, it is important to make a plan and adjust it to changing circumstances, but all parties must trust it enough to make sure it is fully implemented.

Reason #2: A Little Knowledge Is a Dangerous Thing

This boils down to the fact too many advisors don't know what they don't know. Sometimes they fail to get the facts. Other times they give advice without them.

I was referred to another family business by an outside accountant to an owner who wanted to increase his life insurance. For typical life insurance agents, this would be music to their ears — you can't have too much life insurance, right? However, it prompted me to ask questions that would reveal the underlying reason for more coverage and to analyze the right policy and ownership structure to get the most value.

Most business owner plans are piecemeal and act based upon something that was presented to them at the time that seemed interesting, or could save them taxes, etc. This is better than nothing, but creating a vision for your business and your family and then implementing strategies and financial instruments to support that vision helps to ensure that what you put in place or purchase is truly going to meet the needs of the vision you have created. The insurance he was buying was to help fund the tax bill at his death that could force the sale of the company to pay it.

Not unexpectedly, I deduced there was no planning in place to define the reason. It was a cart before the horse — and there was no cart. For business owners and affluent families, the tax treatment of life insurance can make it a more efficient way to fund specific personal and business financial strategies in the context of overall planning goals.

I resolved to get the problems and solutions in the right order. The owner had bought the company from his father, so he was second-generation. He wanted to transfer it at the right time to the third generation, who were currently active in the business.

Instead of buying insurance and waiting for the right moment to employ it, I suggested he commit to the right Ownership Conversion Plan, which would allow him to be ready for any moment with life insurance funding. I got him and the third generation to understand the use of trusts that would protect everyone's interests through the timeframe the father set. The Ownership Conversion was set to unfold over ten years, throughout which the father retained control while decreasing his ownership.

He is now happy as a consultant to the company, while his daughter and son run the business. The current phase of the plan brings the fourth generation into the picture. If you remember the statistics I listed earlier, the company has beaten the 10 percent survival rate for third generation businesses, and enters the virtually unknown territory of a fourth-generation success.

Time Can Be Your Ally

For every business owner who can't buy into the notion of giving up his passion, and every business owner who allows unconscious design to delay conscious design, and every other business owner with a unique excuse, let me assure you there is no reason to avoid Ownership Conversion planning and every reason to engage right now. It multiplies your options and allows you to enlist and leverage what may be your most powerful asset — time.

If you are an entrepreneurial business owner in your 40s or 50s, not only can you avoid a lot of obstacles and missed opportunities with a conversion plan, you also gain control over all the variables and complexities in a measured and consistent manner. That is, if you make this investment and start planning for Ownership Conversion today.

If you are an entrepreneurial business owner in your 60s, your legacy goals still have excellent odds for success. The design decisions you could have made and implemented five years ago are still waiting for your attention, and your destinations will not necessarily be harder to reach.

However, they need your priority attention — more deep drilling, less advice-seeking on the golf course and racquetball court, and a strict moratorium on what-if exercises destined for rabbit holes. Don't waste your time and energy—the investment in Ownership Conversion value is primary.

If you are an entrepreneurial business owner in your 70s or early 80s, you are not out of the game yet. Possibly a few more years of deferred retirement and a healthy measure of flexibility will be required, but most of the actions you need to complete can be fast-tracked with the right advisor team.

Reason #3: Business Owners Can't Buy Into the Vocabulary

Seriously? Yes! The messages advisors use to get you to plan ahead are misguided and uninspired.

Let's say you founded your business a couple of decades ago based on one 'aha' experience — one brilliant idea for a product or service that would solve a nagging problem for consumers or businesses. In effect, you gave birth to a solution and nurtured it through the early development challenges with the same care as a child needs. Your business grew and expanded and matured based on your leadership and your decisions.

Now some business attorney or business banker or business broker or business coach comes along without ever having built a business. They all ask the same question: Do you have an "exit" plan.

Exit? Meaning walking away from everything you created. Saving you from all the stress. Assuring you retire in style.

Inspiring? Not to any business founders I know. Leaving their business is tantamount to losing their business, abandoning their customers and employees, taking away all the fun and replacing it with simply getting older. Exit isn't a plan; it's a guilty verdict with a life sentence.

How does "endgame" strike you? Films, books, music, even sports seem to love the drama in this made-up word. But it started with chess — the plays you have left when all but a few pieces are left on the board. And that is the complete opposite of the ideal for any business owner destinations.

Business "succession" is the most common label. Everybody uses it even though it still carries the taint of "The King is dead!" followed by the crowning of his replacement and a new shout of "Long live the King!" The true spirit of family or protégé Ownership Conversion is not about loss and replacement, but about a prudent and foresighted design for multigenerational integration and collaboration.

What about the term business "continuity?" It has a nice positive feel to it, until you realize that continuity means nothing more than sustaining the status quo. What's there to plan? Besides, entrepreneurs break the boundaries and leave the ordinary behind.

Here is what I want business owners to hear. Ownership Conversion is the ultimate *growth* challenge for entrepreneurs — one requiring you to set destinations and design the strategies and actions that can take you there. Let me repeat the inspiring part of that sentence. Growth. What has been your objective every year you have been in business? Growth.

Don't get caught by these negative messages about exiting and giving up control. Stay focused on what you always have focused on: Growth. But this time, design that growth for maximum Ownership Conversion value whether the destination is an outsider sale, an insider sale, or a family sale.

When I design Ownership Conversion Plans, every component has a positive impact on your growth today. Every change for the sake of Ownership Conversion is a change that can make your company more profitable today, not just more attractive to the next owner several years from now.

What is going to make your company most valuable to an outside buyer? Healthy, reliable, broad growth potential. They are buying a cash cow to turn it into a herd of cash cows.

What's going to make your management team want to take over your company? A strong foundation allowing for potential expansion into new products and new markets. They want to reengineer your vision to fit a changing economic landscape.

What is going to assure financial security and family harmony across generations? Perpetual growth that integrates the interests of active and non-active family owners.

Takeaways

- A consciously designed Ownership Conversion plan will result in the growth of your business and bottom line.
- The messages advisors use to get you to plan ahead are misguided and uninspired.
- An Ownership Conversion plan multiplies your options and allows you to enlist and leverage what may be your most powerful asset — time.

Chapter 4

Know Your Destination

"When a man does not know which harbor he is headed for, no wind is the right wind"
— Seneca

The first objective of Ownership Conversion planning is to reach a clear understanding of your destination. But it's rare to hear an immediate and informed answer from a business owner who is asked to answer that one quick question.

When I work with business owners, I cannot offer advice until I understand their goals and aspirations, their past experience and present circumstances, their successes, their failures, and their lessons learned.

So, rather than corner you about your destination, I would want to learn who you are and what you've done, what drives you, and what slows you down. I want to know how you think, when to support you, and when to challenge you. As you take stock, here is a partial list of what you will need to assess:

- **Vision:** What is your vision of your ideal future for you, your family and your business? What do your heirs want and how do they see their role, let's say 15-20 years out? What income, equity, security will you need to realize that vision?

- **Motivation:** How involved do you want to stay in your business: a full-time commitment, stay connected for a period of time, or just cash out and move on to your next adventure?

- **Capability:** Do you have any personal or business commitments that can or will impact your planning goals?

- **Security:** What are the financial resources you have at your disposal currently, and what will we need to meet your retirement goals and the lifestyle needs of you and your spouse and family?

- **Contingency:** Do you have the necessary planning in place to protect you, your family and your business if the unexpected happens?

- **Value:** Do you know the true value of your business today, and how to structure planning to maximize its value to you and your family? How well do you understand the financial impact of the various ways of liquefying your business value?

- **Variables:** Are we planning to sell to third party buyers, to inside buyers, or to transition the business to the next generation? Or a combination of both?

You Will Need a TEAM

Talking with business owners about engaging a team of advisors will cause most to hide their checkbooks. Add to the dread of paying fees the chronic entrepreneurial preference for autonomy and resistance solidifies. I've seen the thousand-yard stare many times.

But Ownership Conversion is about selling your life's work on your terms to outsiders, insiders, or family members. It's not a Do It Yourself project, unless your business just happens to be an Ownership Conversion advisory firm. Your Ownership Conversion will be a strategy comprised of many plans that will be active and require ongoing attention right up to your date of sale or transfer to the next business leader(s).

Your planning team covers specialized expertise and experience that business owners can rarely duplicate with their inside talent — and seldom with outside advisors trusted to assist with ongoing business concerns. Your planning team functions as your knowledge sources, teachers, counselors, and coaches.

But the most important aspect is always "team." In addition to the diverse experience they bring, they must be collaborators and communicators, keeping you and their colleagues reactive and proactive as plan and implementation evolve.

What the team needs from you is a commitment to listen up, to ask questions, to challenge assumptions and conclusions — in short, be a good student. In return, the team's commitment is to maximize Ownership Conversion value in any scenario you choose. And you control the choosing.

Your Core Team should include a Financial Advisor, your CPA, and your corporate legal counsel. There will be, or may be, others who need to be pulled in for various tasks by your Core Team, and I have listed below who some of these may be. However, your core team should be doing all the heavy lifting, making your involvement easy and not exceptionally time-consuming.

Your Financial Advisor: The Financial Advisor should have solid experience in constructing ownership conversion plans. They will be the Big Picture part of the equation, helping you determine your objectives and financial ability to meet these objectives. This individual will tend to be the lead advisor who ensures that the process moves along and that all advisors are openly communicating and working together as a team and covering all the necessary planning. The Financial Advisor also will be your prime contact during this process.

Your Certified Public Accountant (CPA): What your accountant delivers is transparency with a detailed analysis of your past and current financial and tax performance, and of future strategies to maximize the value of your company. Outside buyers always send in their own teams to verify the seller's financial strength, and offers go down or up based on what they find. Inside sales to employees and family members are seldom contentious, but all buyers want to avoid surprises. Having a CPA who knows what they are looking for protects the value of the company and stabilizes emotions during the Ownership Conversion.

Your Legal Counsel: What you get from the business attorney and the estate attorney is a strong foundation for the Ownership Conversion Plan. Attorneys structure the transfer of business ownership and the transfer of estate assets in accordance with legal and regulatory standards. They can assemble all the pieces in an integrated set of comprehensive agreements and trusts, drafted to clarify and quantify obligations, prevent errors and omissions, protect interests, and preempt conflicts.

Pulling It Together

I had the privilege of working with a client who had a few solid professional advisors and access to the best-in-class advisors for decades. This client is and has been exceptionally successful in building businesses and enterprises that most of us only encounter in our dreams. In spite of that, his Ownership Conversion planning was among the worst I have ever seen! His sole focus was on managing and growing what he had created and worked in his business, not on the business and what the future would look like without him.

Through my persistence, I was able to get all the advisors working together as a team and make real progress toward securing his current assets and structuring an orderly transfer of business and personal assets in the future. As a team, we worked behind the scenes evaluating and beating up all the options the client had, discussed pros and cons of alternative strategies, and coming up with optimal scenarios for the client. This all lead up to a meeting with the owner and his family where options were presented.

Together, we saved the family tens of millions of dollars in unnecessary taxes and settlement costs. More importantly, the end result was that our mutual client knew that all his trusted advisors were on the same page, viewed all options from their unique perspectives, and then agreed on appropriate actions. This made the eventual client buy-in much simpler and more effective.

In this case as all cases, *team* proved to be the word that made the difference. It takes a team of trusted advisors to ensure that all the bases are considered, debated, and addressed to the benefit of the client and those who depend on them. No matter how solid your advisors seem to you, if you fail to keep them informed and functioning as a team, you are wasting resources and undermining their value to you.

I have provided below a list of professionals who possibly may be required in addition to the Core Team for business owners who want to prepare their companies for the ultimate strategic growth triumph. As you go through the list, you see an endless chain of invoices for professional services. Let me counter that legitimate thought with one from an astute accountant: *Everything looks expensive until you compare it to something.*

Your Core Team will determine which other professionals may need to be brought in during the process to ensure a successful outcome, based on the planning and supplemental needs.

Corporate Finance: Many successful small businesses have been cruising for years without the need for strong financial management. Outside buyers know this and can take advantage of owners in a sale. To prepare for all models of Ownership Conversion, input from a temporary outsourced CFO can add significant value by helping an owner develop financial management policies, or system platforms and applications, specific to your needs and of the type that sophisticated outside buyers will seek. In other words, they will help you plug holes that buyers may point to as a reason for under-valuing your business.

Valuation Specialist: When business owners tell me they have been approached by buyers, they typically say the offer was far too low to consider. When I ask them to estimate the value of their companies, I expect the answer to be high. Whatever sale destination you are aiming for, professional valuation gives both sides a realistic starting point, with specific reasons for a valuation linked to real market comparables and specific strengths/weaknesses in your business. A solid valuation will also help to highlight a possible punchlist of things that might need to be addressed to improve the value of the business.

Life Insurance Planning: Life insurance historically plays an important role in Ownership Conversion planning. Policies are structured to resolve continuity risks, fund tax liabilities, provide asset liquidity, and enhance executive compensation strategies. However, only a small segment of the insurance agent population has the advanced knowledge, experience, and resources to provide such comprehensive advice for business Ownership Conversions. Your Financial Advisor many times may have this core talent.

Merger & Acquisition Planning: Many business owners assume M&A specialists are only interested in big transactions between large private businesses and even larger ones. Yet, small- and medium-sized private businesses also attract investor capital, and M&A firms can play an important role in connecting buyers and sellers. No one is closer to what attracts buyers, how to evaluate sellers, and when the timing is right.

Human Resources Compliance: From the labor abuses of the Industrial Revolution to the management abuses of this political correctness era, Human Resources has evolved into a liability monster for private businesses. It takes a master of federal and state regulations to protect you from violations, penalties, and lawsuits as you prepare your company for sale. Again, if this aspect of your business is perceived to be a weakness by a potential buyer, it will degrade the valuation of it.

Risk & Liability Management: There is no such thing as business-as-usual when it comes to risks and liabilities. From environmental concerns to employee safety, from longstanding contracts to short-term contingencies, you probably don't realize all the risks and liabilities that threaten your company — or its potential value. After assessing all of this, a risk specialist can help you analyze complex choices of when to retain risk or shift it to insurers.

Executive Team Development: In every Ownership Conversion scenario, the effectiveness and loyalty of your top employees will be challenged. Entrepreneurs are equally known for inspiring loyalty and undermining autonomy. Meanwhile, they rely on outmoded compensation strategies that fail to align the personal financial goals of executives with the corporate financial goals of the company. These are very important people in any conversion, since they are the people who any buyer will count on to carry on the venture after a sale or conversion. If they disappear, or appear to be at risk of either leaving or being incapable of effective management, the value of your business drops.

Technology Management: Outside buyers are careful not to pay for businesses where technology problems must be fixed. Replacing legacy systems, integrating standalone systems, inheriting homegrown techs and outmoded operations hardware — all can raise red flags. On the other hand, clean and efficient systems from the factory floor to customer relationship management to corporate finance can add a premium to acquisition offers.

Family Business Counseling: Communication obstacles and emotional baggage within the family have a way of festering in the family business. Many sons and daughters grow up resenting how the business always came first, undermining multigenerational ownership aspirations. Or, children active in the business may find themselves in conflict with non-active siblings over business decisions. Professional family business counselors have heard it all and their experience can prevent problems and prescribe solutions.

Owner Wealth Management: Whether the revenue from a business sale comes in one check, as an income stream over years, or as repayment of a loan, two goals must be achieved: Minimize the tax impact of the Ownership Conversion event, and maximize the value of assets outside to the business. Once any form of sale is implemented, you need to engage in personal wealth management planning to protect and preserve family financial security and harmony over generations.

The timing of when — or if— you should bring in certain professionals is solely dependent on your particular circumstances. Each business is unique from this perspective and your core advisory team will help you decide on who should be brought in and when. Your core advisory team should be comprised of a financial/business succession professional, your CPA, and your corporate attorney, at a minimum.

Are You Ready?

So, okay: Let's assume right here that you are convinced that having an Ownership Conversion plan in place is a good idea.

Let's also assume that you now can see the scope of what needs to be scrutinized, tweaked, modernized, and talked out, and admit that you would be most unwise to try to tackle the task yourself, or even with the advisors who have helped you build your business over the years.

And let's finally assume you have taken some time to at least begin to peer into the mist and give some tangible shape to what you would like life to become once you transition from business owner — to something else.

Hooray, for that is the hard part for most business owners — to pull their heads up from the task at hand and to recognize they must assemble a plan to effectively get themselves, their business, and those who depend on them to that new personal and organizational destination.

In the next part, I help you tackle some of the real nuts and bolts of the plan you now know you need.

Part Two

7 Key Steps to a Sound OCP

SELLING TO outside buyers, other shareholders, a management team, or family members all share a common foundation — your commitment to growth. Without a history of growth and current healthy growth, it's difficult for a potential buyer to see the projected growth that makes your company valuable. Yet each designed destination — outside or inside Ownership Conversion — will be different because the variables are different.

Since day one, your company's success has been measured by growth. Growth is proof that you made and executed good decisions. It's proof you can react and adapt to obstacles. Proof that your company's future is bright.

So you must prove to your company's next owners that growth is your first priority up to the day your Ownership Conversion Plan is executed.

Of course, there are many variables that potential buyers analyze, with different weight given to each by each type of buyer. Growth may be the primary buyer motive, but any of these variables can be deal-killers. So, depending on the destination or destination alternatives you choose, you must uncover the weaknesses in your company from a buyer's point of view and convert them to strengths. In other words, much of the design work and time investment will be directed to controlling the variables, accentuating your strengths and removing your weaknesses as a candidate for sale.

All business owners part with their businesses voluntarily or otherwise. All owners want to receive — or have their heirs receive — the maximum amount of money when the business changes hands. As the most tangible reward for entrepreneurial creativity and persistence, the money is an important measure of success.

No less important is the psychic satisfaction that business success makes a difference, and that personal, family, and legacy goals can be achieved. All these potential dividends make your destination worthy, and all should be incorporated in the design of your Ownership Conversion Plan. A written plan — because a plan that is not documented is nothing more than a wish.

Your Ownership Conversion Plan will help you design every element that will move you most efficiently from where you are today to your Ownership Conversion event. All the resources you require will be accessible. All the variables can be controlled. All the unintended consequences can be resolved. Your destination choices can be waiting for you.

In this part of my book, I offer you seven Ownership Conversion Plan design essentials to reach your destination. It would be convenient to check these off one-by-one in a linear progression. However, the decisions and implementation guided by the seven design essentials are in motion throughout the process. Your advisor team can monitor progress, alert you to needed corrections, and integrate changes to keep your plan current. Entrepreneurial business owners are used to balancing, flexibility, and adaptation. If it was all simple and smooth, successful entrepreneurs would not be such an exclusive group.

As you plan for this future, don't lose sight of the fact that you also are improving your present operations. There is a significant present benefit to ownership conversion planning.

So don't think only in terms of the future impact of all the design tasks. Everything you do for ownership conversion will make your company more efficient and more profitable today. Your Ownership Conversion Plan converts tomorrow's coming success into an asset providing greater success today.

Takeaways

- Without addressing all 7 OCP steps with a plan for Growth, present and future there is no successful Ownership Conversion.
- You will experience Growth to Your business bottom line and greater success today as a result of this planning.

CHAPTER 5

CEMENT YOUR FUTURE VISION

"The best time to plant a tree was 20 years ago. The next best time is now"
— **Chinese Proverb**

AN INVESTMENT client of our firm called me for advice one day recently, explaining that someone had made a good offer to buy his company and he wanted to know what I thought. The excitement in his voice told me he wanted to make this happen — if the price was right.

I had performed limited work with him up to this call, so I had too little knowledge of his business to evaluate an offer. But that didn't mean I had no help to give him.

I cleared time on my schedule for a meeting during which I asked him two questions: Was the price attractive to him and did he believe the transaction would be clean? He said yes to both, adding that he wished he knew what similar businesses had sold for so he could compare this offer to others. Obviously, he was going to have second thoughts no matter what happened.

The value of any business, like the material value of any object, is determined by what buyers are willing to pay for it at a specific point in time. The best way to determine what buyers are willing to pay is to create an auction and get multiple bids. A single bid most often will not draw your best offer.

Furthermore, a seller may not know the reasons a buyer is interested in purchasing a business; e.g. acquiring clients, market penetration, income, economies of scale, assets, strategic value. Attracting the most bids a seller can get from a diverse pool of potential buyers is the most proven method for yielding highest valuations.

Most business owners I know have a figure in mind of what their companies are worth. Some of these values might be what they hear others are getting, or assumed multiples of gross or net income, or maybe based on an article they read in the media. Yet, professional advisors I know engaged in Ownership Conversion planning privately roll their eyes at these numbers. Almost all owner estimates are high. A few are low. Rarely are they realistic either way, because the value of a business cannot be determined simply from the owner's experience and intuition.

However, I didn't challenge the offer. Instead, I congratulated him for proving his entrepreneurial success, and admitted I couldn't advise him about the value of his company based on what I knew. Then I added that there was another, much simpler, comparison that would tell him very clearly whether this was an opportunity to push along or not.

That intrigued him, so I told him to think through the personal financial plan we had developed for him. Did he remember the net amount of money he needed to achieve his retirement lifestyle and his family's financial security?

He took a deep breath. The number rolled out from his lips and hung in the air. He realized the offer from the phone call was 40 percent below his retirement need. I asked him what else he could liquidate to make up for the value of his company. Nothing that valuable.

I quickly reassured him that, if he stayed the course with his financial plan, his retirement and financial security goals could be achieved. Only, right now, income from the business was driving that plan, so the price for the company had to cover his current financial needs as well as his retirement funds.

On the other hand, if we began designing his Ownership Conversion Plan, we could work to make the business more attractive to a buyer. He agreed with me, we went to work and implemented the design essentials, and within one year his profits grew by $1 million.

One solid lesson we should take from this. No matter how much pride you feel in your company, no matter how much money someone else is ready to pay to own that pride, you should not be tempted to sell or buy with so little information. You must have a *realistic* idea of what you can expect to get back when you sell your business.

A second lesson is more important. Know your destination. Know the financial parameters that must be met in order to support it.

Get Ready for 'Gap Shock'

What's the first obstacle you will encounter in this planning process? Gap Shock! Gap Shock is the difference between what you *feel* your company is worth, and what buyers *know* it is worth.

Gap Shock applies primarily to selling the business to outsiders, but it can just as easily cause difficulties in negotiations with internal buyers and family successors. Here are the two sides of the gap and the reason Gap Shock exits.

Your buyers will be sending in valuation experts who will pore over the information you must give them. The strengths they encounter will add to your company value. The weaknesses they locate become negative value components. It's all cut-and-dried to analysts.

They will see things differently from how you see them and put importance on things you never thought about. A few of these can be found below:

- What is your long term strategic plan/vision for the business? How is this plan being implemented, measured and modified, when required? Does this vision take into consideration market, technology, and demographic changes on the horizon that can impact your business?

- Who are the key players who will stay with the company after you are gone? How have you assured they will stay and by what methods?

- Can your business truly run effectively and profitably without your involvement?

- How effective is your Human Resource component, and how is this measured and confirmed? Do your employee benefit plans and compensation structure enhance or work against optimal performance of those the company depends on?

- How well-documented are your systems and structures that support your business?

- Do you have a solid method of overseeing and optimizing your business finances? What checks and balances does your business employ for this purpose?

- Are your revenue sources diversified or are they dependent on a few large customers/clients?

They also will compare your company to recently sold companies that you might not think have any relevance to your company. Eventually, they will test their analysis in an up market or down market. They will look at recent sales just as a Realtor would look at recent comparable sales of houses like yours before establishing a listing price.

The number all this generates could strike you as heartless. Regardless, that's how they *know* what your company is worth. Buyers are going to want to buy a company based on the most recent 2-3-year profit & loss statements. Sellers should sell the business based on the future; i.e. add what is in the pipeline, annual sales growth, etc.

Furthermore, the financials should be recast so that expenses that business owners typically allocate to the business are deducted: The owner's entire salary or above-market salary, depending on how involved he/she is in operating and growing the business; owner's car; key man insurance; owner bonuses; charitable contributions, etc.

Meanwhile, you may be thinking about how dramatically the company has grown and earnings have compounded with you at the helm. But you won't be at the helm, so what seems like the-sky's-the-limit to you looks like pie-in-the-sky to them, and your buyer will discount your projections accordingly.

Forget how you started the business decades ago with a revolutionary idea in a symbolic garage. It might have failed right then and there, had you not put in the long days and weekends. And all the investments you made to win over customers, employees, suppliers, distributors, bankers. There must be value in all that effort and risk-taking and perseverance. That's part of what you *feel* your company should be worth.

Who is going to win that debate? The one who *knows* or the one who *feels*?

Not many business owners negotiate a favorable outcome to the gap on their own. And that isn't the only gap in Gap Shock. Here are some more examples.

- There could be a very uncomfortable gap between the cash funding of your retirement lifestyle and the cash proceeds generated at the time of sale.
- There may be a gap between what you believe your life expectancy to be and the added years medical science is giving you — raising your retirement income needs.
- And if your spouse gets the longevity bonus but you don't, there may be a gap between what you leave for your spouse and what it takes to sustain financial security and family harmony.
- Finally, consider the gap between what you think you might have to pay in taxes from the sale and what the IRS knows you will owe.

Maybe, like most entrepreneurs, you are a genuine optimist. Maybe your positivity and enthusiasm will help you close Gap Shock. So, you decide to wait and see. Well, you can see where I'm going with this. Believe me, the gap is there now and will be there — and much wider with no time to close it — when Ownership Conversion reality meets optimism, positivity, and enthusiasm.

Gap Shock isn't just disappointing. It can be devastating. But Gap Shock can also serve to generate a punchlist of what needs to be done now and over time to remove the negatives the valuators might see. These also are some of the things that can not only grow the sale price, but also enhance productivity and profitability now – which I mentioned earlier. I routinely ask business owners when we begin working together to estimate the value of their businesses. The number is always a little loose, sometimes hallucinatory. But I never feel I should challenge their answers, because any number is achievable when you plan and have time and commit to a planning process with the right advisory team.

What GAP Shock Is and Where It Can Impact You

Your Personal Gap Analysis

GAP Shock takes on many forms, including on a personal level with the annual after-tax cash flow you would need to retire today, or the value of the assets you have accumulated outside of your business.

What about the emotions you feel when you think about retirement and how you balance work and family, health and stress, both material and spiritual. What lessons does your founder's story have for those in your business and family? What level of interest is there in the next generation to take the business forward?

You may think the answers to these questions are one thing, but a frank examination may show them to be quite something else.

Your Business Gap Analysis

There are many aspects of GAP Shock that focus on your business:

- Who you want the business transferred to — family members, co-owners, executives, employees, outside buyers, or some hybrid.

- What your time frame is for relinquishing ownership and control.

- Your thinking about how to grow your business and optimize its value, and your knowledge as an owner about how to receive full value.

- How to design compensation and benefit strategies that will align executives with your business plan and motivate your employees.

- The accuracy and dependability of your company's financial management systems and technology.

- Lastly, the precision and accuracy of your assessment of the current health of the business and its future growth prospects.

Your Assumption Gap Analysis

As individuals, we make many assumptions and these can prove to be a challenge when you are accustomed to the many perks of being an owner rather than supporting these perks as personal expenses. There may be a significant gap between the amount of after-tax cash flow you want, and the ability to meet these desires.

You also may encounter a gap regarding how to instill a sense of stewardship of family assets in your children and grandchildren, and the effective shift of wealth to these same individuals. Or in your assumptions about assuring that your spouse has security and support to continue family harmony for two, three, or more generations.

Or there may be gaps because of faulty assumptions about meeting the expenses related to aging, or about your desires to continue to fund causes and organizations important to you.

Your Support Gap Analysis

Gaps almost always exist when it comes to the support you require to effectively plan and reach your objectives with this process.

There inevitably will be Gaps between the abilities and knowledge of your existing professional advisors, and the many professional resources required by you and your business to complete a successful Ownership Conversion. This can relate to corporate finance, legal, accounting, human resource compliance, technology management. and risk and liability management.

The first step in an effective conversion strategy is to close these gaps, and that can only be done by acquiring and then absorbing the realities at play in each and every instance.

Takeaways

- GAP shock takes many forms — Whatever you guess your company is worth, you are probably high.
- Whatever you think is a good offer from a buyer is probably low.
- The best way to maximize value is to begin Ownership Conversion planning now, fill the value gaps over time, and focus on growth.
- Don't forget to add PH to your plan and create a Personal Hedge.

Chapter 6

The Size of the Pot

Without knowing the current value of your business, we are working with two hands behind our back in developing a credible plan for future Ownership Conversion opportunities.

If you have been courted by buyers in the past, congratulations. Their offers may be useful, but far from definitive for your plan.

The destination you set for when and how you want to withdraw from ownership and control gives us a probable timeline and some of the psychic boundaries to work within. A current qualified valuation of your company then gives us the coordinates you start with.

Understand, though, that even qualified valuations of your business will be an estimate. But this full inventory of your company's assets and liabilities — the value of what you own and what you owe as the owner. It produces a hard number to plan around and reveals soft spots that your plan must correct. In addition, the evaluation also allows us to load benchmarks and time frames into the growth process.

Valuation follows the logic of fair market value. Fair market value sets the price based on what a willing buyer with reasonable knowledge of the facts and no compulsive reason to buy would pay, *and* what a willing seller with reasonable knowledge of the facts and no compulsive reason to sell would take.

Oftentimes when buyers become interested, value can quickly become complicated. And business value, like beauty, lies in the eyes of the beholder.

Strategic buyers who are purchasing proven operations as well as seeking a good fit with their own companies may see synergy and the cost of integration as a subjective value. Their goal is to expand growth and profits long term.

On the other hand, financial buyers are purchasing today's performance with the expectation of near-term returns and mid-term exit, so solid cash flow and leverage create subjective value.

Within your Ownership Conversion team, you will have access to a Certified Valuation Analyst (CVA), either as part of the team or as a resource to the team. It is critical that your team has access and information on all your assets and liabilities, right down to the details of how any liquid assets are invested. All of this will be utilized to evaluate what needs to be done to support your designed destination.

Your business valuation is important not only for an outside sale but also for all Ownership Conversion options.

If your Ownership Conversion Plan assumes an outside buyer — or if you want to keep that option open — your advisor team will perform another current valuation at that time and eventually bring in a business broker or a Merger & Acquisitions advisor, depending on business size and other factors.

If you have inside buyers among your partners, executives, employees, or family, the valuation process is equally important, but the implementation of the inside sale negotiation tends to focus more on time and financial structure than pricing.

Do you have the time to transition family members who may have worked in the business during summers into successors or buyers? If you have family members fully engaged in the business, do you have the time to train and transition them into leaders?

Management team buyers need time to gel as a team and achieve both autonomy and collaboration skills so they can function effectively as partners. Most of the time, management team buyers will not have the same experience, talents, background, instincts, etc., that you have that have helped you to succeed in your business. Therefore, you will likely need to evaluate each team member and their strengths and create the synergies over time to replace all that you bring to the table, then improve upon this over time to allow you to gradually withdraw from day-to-day involvement with the business. Since they probably don't have the cash to purchase the company, the financial structure depends on compensation agreements that create a win-win, which in turn rests on the valuation of the company.

Why a Personal Hedge (PH) Is Important

As you approach a plan, knowing the business valuation is not enough. Your business may be the largest asset in your financial statement, but personal assets also need to be identified and assigned a role in funding your retirement cash needs and legacy goals.

A valuation of personal assets tells the financial advisors on your team how to design an investment strategy to build assets outside the business that are equal to the value of the business and prevent business downturns from disrupting future personal financial security.

I consider Personal Hedge to be an imperative component in reducing or eliminating gap shock for all entrepreneurs. This involves taking full advantage of unique planning opportunities available to private business owners, allowing the accumulation of assets outside of your business that ultimately enables you to achieve the cash flow outcomes and desires you have regardless of the value of the business.

Your Personal Hedge takes full advantage of the benefits of business ownership, and has the IRS in effect contributing up to or more than 50 percent to your plan each year! We have structured plans that can allow for the accumulation of assets outside of your business and allow for qualified business deductions of more than $2 million per year into another entity. These receiving entities can shelter these assets from the full erosion of income taxes, and can grow substantially over time.

Several years ago, I began working with a client whose business was valued at more than $10 million, with net cash flow of $2 million a year. He had only accumulated $1.5 million of assets outside of his business, half of which were tax-deferred retirement funds, which are not uncommon. After evaluating his current and future wants and needs, I determined that he needed net after-tax assets of $10 million to meet his objectives. The primary objective was to allow him to exit his business at the end of five years.

He had six highly valued employees that the business depended on for its current and continued success. Two of these individuals he believed were suited to own and run the business when he was no longer there. While these were the individuals he wanted ultimately to own the business, he could not see how they could realistically purchase it.

So, his wish list included the following goals:
- To realize the net after-tax assets to meet the income desires of the owner.

- Ensure that the key management group would stay on and continue to support and grow the business.
- Structure an Ownership Conversion event that allowed the two key employees to purchase the business.
- Minimize the tax drag on any and all transactions.

Our first solution was to create a hedge for the client. His Personal Hedge would provide more than $1 million a year, deductible by the business and tax-sheltered or tax-deferred for each of the next 5 years. We utilized a combination of a specially structured retirement plan, and another new corporate entity designed to help offset corporate risks and allow our client to keep all the underwriting profits. Both of which reduced the net taxable income for the business each year.

Then we arranged for a sale/gift of discounted interests in the business to the two eventual purchasers. This made them partners entitled to a share in the profits which ultimately went back to our client as part of the transaction. The value of the business was discounted for this purpose, further minimizing any double taxation that normally takes place with a purchase.

These steps made the prospective inside buyers bankable as they sought financing for the balance of the buy-out in year five. In addition, this design helped ensure that the other key players who would not be owners would experience the benefits of ownership without being actual owners. This provided them significant tax-free income as long as they remained as key employees supporting the growth of the business.

To accomplish this, we set up what we refer to as a restricted executive bonus plan, which enabled the company to fund a benefit, deduct the funding each year, and offset any tax consequences to the key employees by making their effective contribution $0. We accomplish this while limiting the employees' access to this cash until a later time, or according to a vesting regimen.

The owner ended up with significantly more than was originally required. The key employees were aligned with the owners' objectives and would be rewarded accordingly as future owners. The plan has now been executed and the owner is enjoying the next phase of his life free of any financial or business concerns.

This Ownership Conversion Plan was also designed to help ensure that any ultimate transfer of assets to the owner's family would be free of the tax man to the greatest extent possible. This was accomplished with solid estate planning taking full advantage of available estate tax credits, and also involved gifting and sales of assets to future generations.

The purchasers now own and control the business, which is running smoothly and successfully today. We ensured that by devising a plan that allowed for a solid and orderly transfer to very capable key employees while keeping the tax cost of transactions at a minimum.

How You Can Do It

It's time to step back and answer some questions. Start with the questions that apply to all of us. Build to the answers unique to you. Discover the implications of your answers so you can carefully quantify and qualify your expectations. Understand what fuels your passion now, what will fuel your future passion, and what it will cost.

Only then can we find the gaps and reverse engineer what will be needed to get you from where you are to where you want to go. Designing your Destinations requires us to fully understand your company's success so we can identify gaps that success may have inadvertently covered up.

Knowing the destination you desire and the value of business and personal assets allows you to design your plan to realistically fulfill your dreams. Having a written plan designed to achieve growth targets by implementing agreed-upon actions can initiate one of the most rewarding and satisfying periods of the entrepreneurial experience.

With such a start, I have watched clients literally sell businesses to outsiders at four times the original value in as little as five years. I also have seen internal sale destinations enable a net asset transfer to inside buyers to come at an increase of 100 percent or more going to the seller with significantly less tax erosion.

With your destination in sight and your valuation in place, you will discover remarkable new clarity in the

Ownership Conversion planning process. With your growth directed toward the destination, controlling the variables no longer feels like a fuzzy idea. Everything starts to have tangible purpose and meaning. Your future — financial security, family harmony, legacy ideals — awaits.

Takeaways

- Getting serious and realistic about designing your company's destination starts with complete financial data.
- You have to quantify future financial security so you can meet your lifestyle, health, and legacy goals.
- With this information, you can wisely initiate the design strategies that will grow your company to the valuation and sale strategies to assure your Ownership Conversion success.

Chapter 7

Turning Your Business Into a Butterfly

What does the next owner of your company want to see? Not the egg, not the caterpillar, not the cocoon. The next owner wants to see a beautiful butterfly.

Below are the major operational variables you, your internal management team, and your Ownership Conversion advisor team need to examine carefully, then design and implement solutions to whatever needs addressing in order to meet buyer standards.

I realize that, as entrepreneurial companies develop, operational decisions are subject to fake-it-until-you-make-it and if-it-isn't-broke-don't-fix-it thinking. Your designed destination can't be reached that way.

When buyers come across typical operational problems, they consider how much they will have to invest to fix them, or how much to lower their offer to compensate for them. You can preempt that choice with solutions implemented today.

Leadership Resources

Entrepreneurs usually come with a surplus of charisma, making them inspirational business generals and tough-love sergeants. They prize and reward loyalty and longevity. Their management teams are willing to put in long hours and would follow them everywhere.

That would seem to be valuable for Ownership Conversion, but it can be deadly. Remember, buyers are not buying you, only what you have built. If it all revolves around you, it probably won't work nearly as well without you. That erodes the business value considerably. If it's going to fall apart without you, it's a problem.

Buyers want something different. For them, loyalty to you is counterproductive. Loyalty to the company is a good beginning, but self-motivation, adaptability, and autonomy are even better. You need to be able to deliver a management team that is excited about the opportunities change brings — not wary about threats and sacrifices after you leave.

Growth isn't measured only by revenues and market penetration. For the management team, growth means elevation from loyalty and following well to accountability and leadership.

Certainly, next owners from outside or inside want to see a committed, motivated, incentivized management team which appreciates that personal financial success is aligned with the company's financial success. If the team itself is your buyer, you wouldn't sell if you doubted their ability. If you have family buyers, they must be confident in your management team.

When was the last time you were in the market for a new home? You probably saw many potentially great homes — if you made an investment to get it the way you would want it. What's rare is a home that suits you perfectly and is move-in-ready. That saves you an expensive rehab. For that you would pay top dollar. A management team that is perfectly suited to or perfectly adaptable to a new owner's needs can make your company move-in-ready!

How do you build leadership out of loyalty? I have met many entrepreneurial business founders who trust their management skills are superior and their micromanagement habits completely justified. Whether they are right or wrong, those abilities have no value to any of the Ownership Conversion destinations—just the opposite.

A mother bear achieves autonomy for her cubs by chasing them up a tree and walking away for good. That sounds brutal, but you may need to make similar changes in your own leadership style slowly over the next few years to get your cubs ready.

What's the longest you have been away from your company before something breaks that only you can fix? A week? A month? An afternoon? If you don't like your answer, you would be wise to add a change management consultant to your Ownership Conversion team. They can help you and your management team navigate the behavioral and emotional issues holding your firm back from the move-in-ready ideal.

Rewarding/Retaining Key Personnel

Buyers also want to see compensation practices that align key employees' personal financial security to corporate financial success. Most private business owners lean toward salary, perks, and discretionary bonuses. That's because they require minimal administration or regulation and can be controlled by the owner.

But they also unnecessarily drain the company's working capital and only minimally incentivize productivity once they become routine and expected. You need to move toward incentives designed to actually motivate key employees and reward specific, measurable results. These fall under one of two headings — equity-based and cash-based. They share four characteristics.

- Specific and known in advance so key employees know what must happen for them to earn the reward. They have a clear understanding of the metrics, and obligation they must satisfy to receive these benefits.

- Tied to performance standards that increase the value of the business — typically cash flow.

- Are substantial in the eyes of the key employees. By substantial, it should be the equivalent of 20-50% of their base salary as incentive compensation.

- Handcuff the employees to the business in a positive way. If they leave the business before a specific time period or violate employment agreements, they can forfeit some or all of the funds.

Cash-based incentive programs include cash bonus, Non-Qualified Deferred Compensation, Phantom Stock plans, Restricted Executive Bonus plans, and Stay Bonus plans. Equity-based incentive plans include Stock Bonus plans, Stock Option plans, and Stock Purchase plans.

Aligning the needs of key employees with the needs of the company with tailored incentive plans can have a great impact on growth and, in turn, on business value. The more personal the plan, the greater the impact on all involved. These plans should be systematic and supported by agreed upon objectives and not subject to the owner's discretion for them to be realized.

I like to start with an understanding of your key employees individually and what is important to them on a personal and financial level. Then I tie that to a plan that will serve their needs and desires and that directly benefits the business' bottom line and future value.

Most of the unconscious planning that traps entrepreneurial businesses is due to the owners not understanding what the real issues and real solutions are, and misguidedly assuming these solutions are unnecessary and overly complex.

A company I referenced earlier closed its doors many years ago due to mistakes of unconscious planning. They left their business with no Ownership Conversion Plan other than the directive that ownership be passed down to all the children of the owners, regardless of whether the children were active in the business or not.

When the Ownership Conversion took place, there were close to twenty owners, no vision, no direction, conflicting interests, and a management team that collapsed under the weight of indecision and lack of empowerment.

What if the original owners had the foresight to create financial incentives and reporting systems that would help the management team keep the ship running, even with so many owners, instead of running aground? What if a management plan gave the team the resources and responsibilities to operate the business as only they knew how to do it, then rewarded them for successful outcomes?

That alone would have accomplished two very desirable results. The business would still be operating successfully today, and the heirs would have continued to benefit financially whether or not they were active owners. Maybe the business could have been prepared for an outside Ownership Conversion event in which all parties, including the management team, could have benefitted.

What if a business has no family Ownership Conversion opportunity and a sale to the management team is not viable? Then the owner loses the ability to operate the business due to disability or death. There may still be Ownership Conversion opportunities with outside buyers, but only if the management team and other key employees don't depart as well. A company with no leadership is not very valuable to most buyers.

But how can the management team be motivated to at least see it successfully go through that transition?

Bonus Plans

My own team has put in place what we call a Stay Bonus plan designed to provide for a big payoff in cash to key team members who remain to see the business through such a transition. The plan can guarantee that the cash will be there to meet that obligation, so the designated key employees know the funding is there, not simply projected to be there.

Another example of a plan that we have used on several occasions to reward and tie key employees to a firm is called a Restricted Executive Bonus Plan or REBA, which offers the following benefits for owners and buyers.

- You can pick and choose the key employees you include in such a plan.
- Contributions to the plan can be tailored to each individual key employee.

- Contributions can be tax deductible to the company today, over time, or at the time of distribution.

- The plan can provide for an income tax-free distribution upon the death of a key employee to beneficiaries designated by him or her.

- It is possible to structure a plan so that it is cost neutral to the key employee — costs them nothing out of their pocket.

- You can restrict access to the assets in this plan until a future date and even put in a vesting schedule.

- Assets in the plan for each employee can accumulate income tax deferred.

- If properly structured, the income distributions from the plan to the key employee upon retirement can be income tax-free.

If you started now to redirect leadership commitment toward greater autonomy and more responsive incentives, would it have a strong impact on the company's growth even today? You bet!

Human Resources Management

Business founders preparing for Ownership Conversion today may have started their businesses when HR functions included an employee handbook and some training slide shows. Now HR management is an industry of its own with new regulatory requirements and revisions every year. Political correctness, self-identification, and social justice movements are not exactly the business owner's friends.

Outside buyers do not want to pay for problems. When their due diligence team sees an HR office with two administrators and files stacked on top of dusty cabinets next to a cactus in a pot, they fear the worst. Noncompliance equals lawsuits, and lawsuits beget more lawsuits. HR and other people issues are frequently cited reasons for mergers and acquisitions failing to meet expectations.

HR planning should begin with an inventory to assess effectiveness and compliance in your hiring, onboarding, training, and severance policies. Next, evaluate your employee compensation and benefit programs, retirement plans, and health and welfare plans to identify the impact on profitability, competitiveness, and company culture.

When I ask business owners what their company's most valuable asset is, many of them say without hesitation, "my employees." You know very well how human capital can make or break your business.

Put yourself in the position of a potential buyer, internal or external, If the HR house is not in order, would you pay full price or negotiate down? I have walked into businesses for the first time and had my hair figuratively stand up on the back of my neck as I saw the mess that was their HR function — if *function* is a word that can be used. Any buyer would see the same problems.

A client who recently engaged us was taking all possible shortcuts to save costs in the HR area. They were funding their benefit offering as a start-up organization might, paying the minimum possible for medical and offering minimal supplementary benefits. Our assessment clearly showed they had a very dissatisfied employee pool that was impacting the bottom line. Pennywise, pound-foolish, but the owner couldn't see it that way.

They saw only a lack of appreciation for what the company did provide. They were right in the sense that employees were not appreciative of the larger take-home pay made possible because of the poor benefits they were paying for. Of course, we appreciate that private businesses have been hammered by cost increases for decades, but having a lack of appreciation thrown in can leave a bitter taste.

We encouraged the owner to think beyond cost saving and consider a different approach that could reward him with much higher appreciation and raise the cost of benefits to the company by only 10 percent. We restructured the benefit offering in a way that the employees truly appreciated and valued, and met the 10 percent target. The result over time was an enhanced bottom line and increased value for the company.

However, the most satisfying change was the difference between our initial employee survey at the beginning of the project and one following implementation, in which the appreciation was extremely encouraging. Now the company is positioned to attract and retain employees with more skills and experience, leverage better morale to meet bottom line objectives, and increase productivity through reduced attrition.

Are these solutions likely to help more private business employers say their greatest asset is their people, today and for the future? Absolutely.

Financial and Legal Management

The due diligence team evaluating your business wants to see three years' worth of financial information at a minimum to determine if growth and cash flow is reliable. You want them to see a history of consistent cash flow, growth and sustainable earnings to prove the future potential of your company. Buyers buy the past; if the business is on a good trajectory, sellers should be selling the future.

A pro-forma should be done to reflect growth over the next two years. Some of the growth will occur through price increases or upselling to current customers. Much of this growth is going to be a result of work you did to build your sales pipeline. Sellers should recast the numbers to eliminate "owner expenses" made to reduce tax liabilities and projected revenues. If a buyer is reluctant to pay for this now, then an earn-out option should be in the definitive purchase agreement to capture the increased profits the buyer will gain from work you have already completed.

Either way, if your financial records, documentation, and reports don't give those impressions, your credibility as a seller sinks. No matter how compelling the founder's story may be, no matter how you managed to survive and thrive over the decades, your financial story is the one that adds up. When you sold the first car you owned, you probably realized the wisdom of wiping up the oil stains underneath it. The same insight applies. Clean up, don't cover up your financial oil spots — at least three years' worth.

Here is another example of a loyalty trap. Many founders get by with simple bookkeeping practices in the early years. As financial management becomes more complex, one of the first management hires is someone with more financial background and experience. Time goes on and formal financial planning and controls are in order, moving that person out of his or her comfort zone. But loyalty by now is firmly established, and the owner hesitates to bring in a foreigner CFO out of consideration for all the years of service. That's nice, but there might not be that much room for sentiment in the Ownership Conversion process. You need to face the need for a more-advanced corporate financial experience internally or obtained by outsourcing.

Another perception problem lies in one of the great advantages of business ownership — that reasonable costs that would otherwise be personal expenses can be paid by the business. In addition, there may be one-off expenses you have incurred during the past three years that should be excluded in a buyer's analysis of recurring cash flow, such as relocation or nonrecurring legal fees. Make certain you have supporting documentation for every example so that a buyer clearly sees what he is buying and not buying.

Finally, the last thing you want to expose to a buyer's due diligence team is significant corporate debt. While you have the benefit of time, address debt issues now and implement a plan to be debt-free before seeking Ownership Conversion opportunities.

Legal considerations are equally important in the due diligence process. Buyers want to see appropriate governance, who has authority to make specific types of decisions, incorporation papers, permits, licensing agreements, leases, customer and vendor contracts, and any other agreements and relationships that might create liabilities or risks for business operations and profitability. Intellectual capital and proprietary technology also must be heavily protected in today's hacking environment. For many service companies, these are likely to be the most valuable assets and the most significant value drivers.

You know you need to put your financial and legal house in order for the due diligence process, but do these steps buy you anything today? No doubt.

I had a client several years ago who agreed to have an analysis of the business operations reviewed by a member of an advisor team familiar with his industry. The analysis discovered that a single change in the method in which jobs were being quoted would reverse a significant loss in revenue to the company. They had been working this way for 20-plus years. Once they made the change, it resulted in an additional $1.5 million to their bottom line each year! We used much of these funds to create a solid PH Personal Hedge strategy for the two owners.

Customer and Product Management

From the day you started your business, a primary focus has been increasing your customer base. And when Ownership Conversion occurs, the new owners — outsider or insider buyers — will have the same priority. For consumer-based businesses and B2B companies, growth depends on customer management, product innovation, and market development.

Customer Loyalty

Customers buy your products once because they solve a problem or create a benefit. Loyal customers buy them again because they trust your products enough to buy more when they need to be replaced. They forgive justifiable price increases, give you five-star reviews online, and recommend your products to others.

They may remain the nucleus of your growth, but by themselves they do not impress your buyers. As amazing as your ability to build customer loyalty looks in the most competitive landscape business has ever known, reliably selling the same product to the same customers is not a reliable history of growth. Plus, it also can be viewed as a vulnerability, if much of your revenue is derived from a handful of long-term customers, or just a few key accounts. This also may mask the lack of any sophisticated sales/marketing operations beyond the owner's charisma, networking, and skill. Not a plus for any buyer. Again, buyers will want to see turnkey systems for these things.

Look at the restaurant industry over the past few decades. Locally successful restaurants were launched across America from the 1960s to the 1990s. Naturally, they chose to grow by opening new locations in their area. Some became regional growth successes and eventually were acquired or attracted capital partners to go national.

Meanwhile, tastes evolve and people look for new foods and new eating experiences. New restaurant concepts have taken over, and while the old favorites still attract loyal customers, it feels like closures may be exceeding openings. The new players quickly build customer loyalty through social media and expand in new ways.

Shopping malls used to feature identical food courts and put store names in lights outside for differentiation. Now they put restaurant names in lights outside for differentiation and feature the same stores as every other mall.

Brand differentiation and market penetration rules have changed. If you feel behind the curve, you might benefit by at least searching the Internet, if not investing in knowledgeable marketing advice, to put you on the right side of the curve for potential buyers.

Product Diversification

Selling the same products to the same customers over and over may not meet the standard for reliable growth. Selling the same products in new locations when access to products is only a click away may not meet that standard either. But selling new products to the same customers is still a growth strategy.

For that you need to innovate and come up with new products related to your current products. Line extension builds on customer loyalty by solving more problems, or by anticipating changing customer desires. From an Ownership Conversion perspective, you need to demonstrate forward-thinking and a willingness to challenge your own status quo with new customer solutions.

Customer Diversification

We are living in a new consumer landscape where American culture has been replaced by countless subcultures. The newest consumer generation is the Millennials, and their consumer mindset is foreign to the Baby Boomers and GenXers who raised them. And while Baby Boom and GenX identify with others within their generations, Millennials aren't a typical "generation" in this aspect. They are more of a maze of subcultures in the same age range.

If your business serves a consistent customer profile, and that profile is declining in numbers, you may want to research other profiles to serve. Your potential buyers

— insiders and outsiders — will appreciate diversification across generations.

Service Reputation

Using social media, today's consumers build relationships with their favorite companies. They respond to interactive opportunities and participate in giveaways. They share their experiences with other users and can become mutual advisors about your products. In contrast, consumers today are increasingly critical of service systems that purposely avoid personal contact. Even lower on the pole are service systems that are outsourced to representatives with weak service skills who are clearly working from scripts.

You always knew that good customer service was important, but service has evolved into marketing. Companies today are expected to interact with the marketplace and invite positive and negative response. Of course, there are risks. As easily as consumers can spread the good word about your company, they can also trash you fairly or unfairly. On the positive side, when customers post negative service experiences, you have an opportunity to fix problems quickly and preserve your service reputation.

Being recognized as a strong player in social media and blogger communities can be an important proof of customer retention when it comes time for an Ownership Conversion.

Operating Systems and Technology

Unfortunately, even when you develop a better way to make or deliver your products and services, you probably won't have that edge for long. Nothing stays unique. Virtually anything can be hacked or pirated. But that's no excuse to hold back and let your operating systems become legacy systems a potential buyer will consider to be something that needs to be upgraded.

Let's expand the meaning of *operating system* beyond software and include everything that supports how the company operates. Potential buyers will not be impressed by old-school systems and outdated technology. Think about these overlooked areas as part of your operating systems:

- What's the impact of a building that looks like it hasn't been rehabbed since the Industrial Age?
- Is the buyer impressed by your desk overflowing with paper and walls covered with 70s graphics?
- Do your manufacturing processes look sleek, and the people who run them engaged?
- Are your company vehicles bright and sassy or rejects from Road Warrior movies?
- Do your office cubicles, computers, and coffee machines have a dreary vintage quality?

When did the last operating systems innovation or renovation occur? When will the next one occur? If you have no expectations, you aren't controlling the variables.

For example, I have a business owner client who thought the method of quoting their jobs was reliable — but only because he always relied on it. As his plan for a future Ownership Conversion progressed, an analyst on his advisor team very familiar with the company's industry discovered a simple modification in the quoting system that enhanced the system dramatically. The approach to quoting that they had utilized for decades was effectively reducing their net profit, due to the method they used to calculate their margin requirements. A very simple figure that went unknown for decades without question. The company improved net profits by 400 percent in one year as a result of the change.

Would innovations and renovations that could lower costs, increase revenues, sustain cash flow, increase profits, and enhance the quality of work for your company be better undertaken tomorrow or today? Make it right today and enjoy the benefits of increased profits today and again at the time of sale through a greater sale value.

Owner Management

If you go back through the topics in this section on how to fulfill your company's potential, they all appear to be decisions you should make and implementation steps that you should control. But that leads to a serious challenge and a challenging question: How important are you to your company?

For most entrepreneurial founders, delegation was probably not an option in the early days. As the company grew, you may have watched a few employees earn levels of autonomy that freed you from absolute oversight. You could say yes to rounds of golf. You could attend industry meetings and other events out of town. Maybe you could enjoy vacations uninterrupted by phone calls, texts, and emails.

But that's not enough. Despite the increased attention to getting your company ready for Ownership Conversion, remember that an outside buyer isn't buying you. Sometimes outside buyers find it prudent to bind you with an employment contract for a period of time when you can consult with the company through its transitions.

You may be among a handful of previous owners who enjoy the relationship, but most of the previous owners I know were apparently born without the employment gene. Their destination is right in front of them, but there is a two-year wait and it's maddening. On the other hand, inside buyers would probably like to have you around — not looking over their shoulders, but embracing an ambassador role for the company within the broader business community.

Owner management is a careful way of saying you need to make yourself unnecessary, irrelevant, disinterested, for a successful Ownership Conversion. Everything about the company that requires your knowledge, experience, presence, or attention could lower the price you should be offered.

Everybody knows you are irreplaceable. But don't take it too seriously. Being *replaceable* this one time can be worth a hit to your ego.

Takeaways

- Designed destinations depend on your buyers' conviction of the value of your business — and you can't hide flaws from them.
- Meeting and exceeding your buyers' expectations requires a deep dive into the weeds of your business with a team of advisors who know how to find and correct every problem.
- Your Ownership Conversion Plan is aimed at your future growth, but has a tremendous positive effect on current growth.

Chapter 8

The Empty Chair

Everything I have presented so far about Ownership Conversion planning has been aimed at growing a business that attracts outsider and insider buyers while maximizing owner control over the price, terms, and timing of Ownership Conversion. All positive goals, but all unattainable without planning for events that could deny you your designed destination.

How do you protect your Ownership Conversion Plan against the possibility that you die or become disabled before the Ownership Conversion event?

That's not even the whole question. In the broadest terms, how can you protect your business, your family, your employees, your suppliers and distributors, your community — anyone who would experience financial loss if your company could not continue without you. For example, if you died or became disabled before your Ownership Conversion Plan is exercised ...

- Can your company continue financially without the support of your balance sheet and your personal guarantees?
- What becomes of company leadership and management and culture?
- What will keep employees from leaving?
- What will keep customers from losing confidence?
- Credit resources? Vendors? Distributors? Retailers? In other words, what happens to trust?

A few pages ago in the section on how to fulfill your company's potential, I wrote that you should make yourself virtually unnecessary and unimportant to the company's success. Yes — for the actual Ownership Conversion negotiations.

But while you are alive and able, you are absolutely necessary to the company's longevity and Ownership Conversion value. You must have a contingency plan in case your longevity is challenged at any time and in any way before the Ownership Conversion negotiations.

Your Business Will

Your business Will — otherwise known as a buy/sell agreement — is one of the most important documents supporting and protecting your business asset and those who depend on it. If you have a formal well-designed buy/sell agreement already, congratulations. Or, rather, if you have one already and you review annually, congratulations. Or, actually, if you have one already that is reviewed annually and is funded effectively, congratulations.

In my experience, very few business owners, including inside accounting and legal professionals who should know better, review the buy/sell document at all. Everybody knows they are not immortal, but on a daily basis everybody thinks and acts as though they are. Everybody knows that changes in business circumstances can impact the buy/sell agreement, but everyone thinks and acts as if the document is written in stone, not on paper.

I have heard the following statements my whole career.

- *We'll be fine.*
- *I have more pressing concerns right now.*
- *Not much has changed.*
- *I'll get to it next month.*

Well, entrepreneurs have a reputation for taking risks. This proves it.

A buy/sell agreement and funding to support it must be reviewed to determine if it still covers the possible problems it was created to resolve. If you need to change it to conform to new circumstances, do it today. If you wait until you need to execute the agreement, you're too late. Your whole investment in Ownership Conversion planning depends on this agreement.

What are you risking?

Here is the outlook for four young shareholders.

Based upon the *Table 2000 Commissioners Mortality Table,* the probability of death of at least one of the four business owners at an age prior to 65.

Age of Shareholder	Percent likelihood that the Shareholder will experience the death of a co-shareholder prior to their age 65
38	37.6 percent
35	46.5 percent
33	52.7 percent
29	65.8 percent

Now consider the probability of a disability for multiple shareholders.

The chances of at least one disability lasting 12 months or longer in a group of two, three, or four owners with an average age between 27 and 52 are shown in the following table.

Probability of a Disability Before Age 65			
	Number of Owners		
Average Age of the group	**2**	**3**	**4**
27	26.3 percent	36.7 percent	45.7 percent
32	25.6 percent	35.8 percent	44.7 percent
37	24.5 percent	34.5 percent	43.1 percent
42	23.0 percent	32.4 percent	40.7 percent
47	20.7 percent	29.4 percent	37.1 percent
52	17.4 percent	24.9 percent	31.7 percent

Disability based on 1985 CIDA, 90-day elimination period, occupation class 1. Statistics vary by occupation. Occupation Class 1: includes professional, technical, and managerial occupations that are generally office duties only.

1985 CIDA is the most current morbidity table for individual disability claim incidence adopted by most State Departments of Insurance

A buy/sell agreement should resolve common risks that challenge business owners by defining what will happen to company ownership, control, and financial management upon the occurrence of key events, primarily your death and your disability — short-term disabilities, long-term disabilities, and permanent disability. It can also specify what happens to your company when you voluntarily withdraw from your leadership position.

It is a common mistake in buy/sell agreements to fail to list and address all restrictions on transfer events during the lifetime of the document and the shareholders. Disability isn't limited to physical conditions. Longer life expectancies may give business owners more time to enjoy the benefits of controlling their companies, but at the same time aging brings on multiple ways in which senility and dementia can take hold. Cognitive impairments must be considered as well as physical disabilities.

Valuation can become a problem as well. Few private businesses review past valuations as a contingency measure. If events trigger the execution of the buy/sell agreement the valuation on which the agreement is based could be so far out-of-date it appears to be for another company.

Another frequent problem is a lack of third-party funding to assure execution of the document without financial hardship for the company, its shareholders, and the deceased owner's heirs. Even when adequately funded, if funding vehicles are not coordinated with the language of the agreement, business operations and financial management may be paralyzed until the issues can be resolved.

What if you are a sole owner and have no co-owner to buy you out if death or disability were to find you? All Ownership Conversion scenarios remain available, as long as you have potential buyers — outsider, management team, family members, employees — as opposed to a fire sale by heirs.

You can also establish a contingency plan with guaranteed financial incentives for key employees who don't abandon ship and stay around long enough to make one of the options a reality. This same planning will provide reassurance for your customer base, employees, vendors, distributors, creditors that your promises made will be promises kept, and that the business has the resources to survive and thrive after your loss.

When an event triggers the buy/sell agreement, the event requires cash to be paid out. Assuming the cash is available, is it better to use cash on hand or to use a third-party payer? What are your alternatives when purchasing shareholders' ownership interest? When considering alternatives, there are those that can cost the purchaser and the seller much more in taxes and business profits to complete the purchase and sale of the business interest. A keen understanding of opportunities to leverage financial instruments and tax planning can dramatically reduce the impact on the business, the purchaser, and the seller.

Cash Funding

- Has the apparent advantage of being simple and requiring no immediate outlay.

- Purchaser does not know precisely when or how much cash will be needed, or who the survivor(s) will be if there are multiple shareholders.
- Purchaser must always keep an adequate cash reserve available
- Where the agreement is in the form of a stock redemption and the corporation purchases the departing or deceased shareholder's stock, corporate surplus, operating capital, or current income will often be drained.

Sinking Fund: Creating a Savings Fund to Provide Cash for a Buy-Out

- If the potential purchaser decides to use cash and establishes a "sinking fund" to meet its obligations under the agreement, can a determination be made as to how much to deposit each year?
- Sinking funds are usually inadequate, because death or long-term disability of a working shareholder is almost always "premature."
- Typically, there isn't enough time or willpower for a business to build up and maintain a sufficient cash reserve.
- The development of a sinking fund may strain or deplete the corporation's working capital.
- The deceased shareholder's family must rely on the financial ability, as well as the moral responsibility, of the purchaser(s).

Borrowed Funds

- Similar to cash, borrowing has the advantages of being simple and requiring no outlay until death or disability occurs.

- Banks may be unwilling to lend money to a business that has just lost a key person who made the corporation what it was.

- If the bank lends the money, the terms and/or rates of the loan may not be reasonable and affordable from the borrower's viewpoint.

- The cash flow required to repay the loan may have a negative impact on operations and credit-worthiness.

Purchase Put Option (PPO) Utilizing Insurance

- This is the only means for guaranteeing that, upon the event of death, the funds are available for a buy-out.

- Premiums can be viewed as advance installment payments that can be budgeted.

- If a buy-out occurs during lifetime, cash values of a policy can be used to help provide a portion of the purchase price.

- Properly structured, income can be taken from the policy tax-free in the event of a buy-out or for retirement.

Now let's evaluate further why third-party funding or creating a PPO — a Purchase Put Option arrangement — can be necessary and desirable.

What Is a Purchase Put Option (PPO)?

A PPO is designed to fund all or part of a purchase obligation and transfer some or all the risk to third-party financial institutions. The third party financial institutions agree to take on this risk for a premium that you will pay them for agreeing to it.

A third-party payer, typically an insurance company ...

- Guarantees the cash will be there to finance some or all the purchase obligation.
- Eliminates or reduces the need for debt obligations associated with a buy-out event.
- Provides tax-free dollars to meet the obligation of the corporation or the co-shareholders.

By carefully analyzing funding needs and policy design, insurance contracts can ...

- Provide cash at death to the purchaser to finance the purchase of a deceased, disabled, or retiring shareholder.
- Provide tax-favored accumulation of cash for a lifetime buy-out.
- Accumulate cash sheltered from taxes.
- Provide cash distributions during life that are structured to be income tax-free.
- Properly structured, enable and support an immediate step-up in basis for surviving owners, even

though they could be utilizing tax-free dollars to fund the agreement.

- Reduce financial stress on a business that just lost an owner key to business success.

Having seen an example of the probability of death or disability with the charts above, it should be clear why third-party funding of contingent buy-out transactions is critical. Third-party funding using life insurance and, when available, disability buy-out funding can be more efficient and cost effective than other funding strategies. Not funding the contingent buy-out purchases can severely restrain your business financially, if you or other shareholders pass away or become disabled while the company is dependent on your leadership.

You can have the insurance to fund a buy-out owned by the business, co-shareholders or an entity owned by all shareholders created to provide access to cash created by the insurance to finance a purchase of stock.

The corporation can redeem the stock of the seller (a Stock Redemption) in exchange for the payment of the purchase price, OR we can have a fellow shareholder purchase the stock from the seller directly (a Cross Purchase). A cross purchase provides the purchaser with a step-up in cost basis, thereby reducing taxes upon the eventual sale of their stock which a stock redemption does not do.

So, let's consider an example for a business valued at $3 million. We have Peter, Paul and Mary as equal shareholders of the business. If Peter were to pass away and his shares now need to be purchased or redeemed, let's look at the impact of Stock Redemption vs. the Cross Purchase.

If Paul and Mary have a cost basis of their existing stock of $250,000 each, and if the shareholders agreement calls for a Stock Redemption by the corporation, the insurance to finance this is owned and payable to the corporation. What will happen is the corporation will redeem Peter's stock and retire it. Paul and Mary will now own the outstanding stock of the company 50/50 and their cost basis will remain at $250,000. If they were to turn around and sell the company they would have a taxable gain of $1,250,000 each.

If, however, the arrangement was treated as a Cross Purchase with the insurance funding outside of the business, Paul and Mary would have the opportunity to purchase Peter's stock AND get an increase in cost basis of $500,000 each, thereby reducing taxable gain on the sale of their interests to $750,000 vs. $1,250,000 — a significant savings in taxes using the same insurance funds in a different manner to structure the purchase. We would have the insurance owned directly or indirectly by Paul and Mary outside of the business, with the agreement obligating them to purchase the stock from Peter or to provide the cash to the corporation to purchase his stock.

There are generally two approaches to consummate a purchase.

Immediate Purchase

- Cash must be available to pay out to the seller at the Ownership Conversion event occurrence.
- Seller or seller's family receives cash immediately.
- No ongoing obligation for remaining shareholders or the business to support payments to the seller.

Installment Purchase

- Apparent advantage of paying over time.
- Ongoing obligation for remaining shareholders and the business.
- Seller's family leaves substantial sums at the risk of future business performance.
- Negative impact on the ability of the business to borrow funds, and reduced capital for reinvestment in the business. An installment purchase does not sever the ties between the business and the family of the departed shareholder, leaving the possibility of survivor impact on management decisions.

In my experience, deferred payments are best reserved as a last resort escape valve if other funding is inadequate, rather than the primary means of financing a buyout at a shareholder's death.

Let's evaluate the options with a recent client example of a Cost of Cash Comparison to purchase a shareholder's interest.

Let's break it down to the cost-per-dollar to purchase a business interest utilizing an installment purchase vs.

funding a purchase with the third-party funding provided by a life insurance funded Purchase Put Option. The following chart assumes that if you have a business that has net before tax income from sales of 17 percent and pays taxes in the top brackets as an S Corp in the state of Connecticut, with a net after-tax cash flow of 8.5 percent.

Let's assume that you now need to pay out a former shareholder for his or her interest in the business. What is the true cost to you considering a dollar paid out today is gone for good. If we have a liability of $1 million what is the true cost of paying this obligation on a per-dollar basis through an installment sale?

If you consider that each dollar expended is a dollar that is not being reinvested in your business (lost opportunity cost) netting 8.5 percent from your business, the true cost is staggering as opposed to paying the costs of insuring the risk with life insurance. All the figures in the illustration below are present-valued back to today's dollars using a 3 percent inflation factor.

Cost per $1	Installment purchase	Funded Buy-out	Cost Reduction
Today	$2.51	$0.01	99.65%
5 years	$2.30	$0.04	98.1%
10 years	$2.03	$0.08	96.03%
15 years	$1.80	$0.11	93.65%
20 years	$1.59	$0.14	90.95%
25 years	$1.45	$0.14	89.76%

The figures above are estimates and should not be construed to be guarantees. Assumptions are that assets remaining in the business earn 8.5 percent net after taxes and all expenses. Inflation assumption is 3 percent for present value calculations. Lost opportunity costs on business assets expended to pay purchase costs assume the above and are present valued back to today's dollars at a rate of 3 percent. Time Period is 20 years.

Let's look at this from a Gross required sale or net profit perspective. This chart evaluates the impact on the business to fund a buy-out using current cash flow based on a current client experience. I am breaking it down assuming a $1 million purchase price

Gross Sales to provide Buy-Out funds for a $1 Million 10-Year Installment purchase		
3 percent Interest	5 percent Interest	7 percent Interest
Today: $6,698,890	$7,400,260	$8,135,860
Total Profits required to Provide Buy-Out funds for a 10-Year Installment Purchase		
3 percent Interest	5 percent Interest	7 percent Interest
Today: $2,344,620	$2,590,100	$2,847,560

Assumptions: 17 percent Average Net Cash Flow, 50 percent tax bracket, For internally funded installment purchase, 3 percent Interest Rate on outstanding balance. Assumption for borrowed funds is a 5 percent Interest rate. Life insurance is the cumulative premiums paid over 15 years. All figures represent the purchase of a single shareholder interest and associated costs thereof.

In summary, a third party financed contingent buy-out utilizing a Purchase Put Option (PPO) Strategy and properly structured can potentially provide the following benefits for the shareholders.

- The PPO guarantees cash will be there to finance some or all of the purchase obligation.
- Cash received in the event of death is income tax-free to the business.
- Surviving shareholders can receive an immediate step-up in basis with proper planning as shared above.
- The need for debt to finance a buy-out is eliminated or reduced.
- Insurance contracts can provide access to cash for a lifetime buy-out, through the cash value that grows inside of the policy. This cash can be accessed by the individual or business that owns the contract.
- Funding of the insurance contracts is flexible and can be increased or decreased as necessary.
- Contracts are portable and can be purchased or distributed to the insured when no longer needed for business purposes.
- Cash accumulation is sheltered from taxes while the insurance policy is active.
- Cash in the insurance contracts can be used to provide tax-free income to shareholders when policies are no longer needed and can be part of a retirement buy-out.

Takeaways

- Any event that takes you out of the picture as the mind, body, and soul of your company amounts to a business suicide.
- A business will can be structured to meet every contingency.
- A carefully and reliably *funded* business can offset the negative financial impact of losing company leadership for family survivors, business partners, employees, and loyal customers.

Chapter 9

Your Personal Hedge

The entrepreneurial instinct is very powerful, and most business founders see their companies as a mission they must fulfill. The financial benefits of owning a business are substantial, as are the efforts to make the business a success. No wonder the largest asset most business owners possess is the business itself.

However, when retirement income and legacy ambitions depend entirely on the continuation and eventual sale of the business, business owners become vulnerable. You don't feel vulnerable, but what if — worst case scenario — your products or services are made obsolete? Unthinkable?

In 2000, Blockbuster Video was at the top of its game. Market share was outstanding. Retail locations numbered in the thousands. Hollywood was at Blockbuster's mercy. The founder and CEO of Blockbuster laughed out of the room the CEO and founder of Netflix when he proposed to form a marketing partnership.

In 2010, Blockbuster Video went bankrupt. Netflix is a multibillion dollar victor, totally obsoleting the video rental infrastructure with its streaming technology.

Between 1955 to 2014, 88 percent of the firms that were once on the *Fortune 500* list are now gone, according to an American Enterprise Institute article dated August 18, 2014. Gone for many reasons, but still gone. Never assume your company is invulnerable, and never ignore vulnerabilities.

My mission is to advise business owners on how to achieve the strongest possible position for the sale of their businesses to outside or inside buyers. Financial strength comes from diversification of financial assets. You need an asset pool outside of the business that can meet most if not all your financial needs at retirement. That's common sense, but too commonly not applied.

What makes my mission satisfying is being able to show business owners how to take full advantage of the benefits of business ownership. They are missing opportunities to leverage business ownership and save very substantial sums of money subsidized to a great extent by funds that would otherwise go down the Black Hole we call the IRS. Once those funds go there, they are gone forever, so here is another application of the theme we started with. Be a lifetime learner. Learn how to use the business to build assets outside of the business.

You probably know you can put excess earnings into a typical qualified retirement plan, but only up to certain limits. As an example, the maximum individual contribution that can go into a Simplified Employee Pension (SEP) or Profit Sharing 401k plan is $54,000-$60,000 annually!

So, what if you want to defer income taxes on amounts higher than $54,000, say $100,000 or $200,000 or more? Most business owners who fit the profiles specified in the tax code don't realize they have that opportunity.

Using the tax code regulating qualified retirement programs, you can combine a 401(k) Plan and a Defined Benefit Plan. This, combined with other solutions and designed correctly, can let you put away sizable amounts of excess earnings — from $50,000 up to as much as $2 million a year sheltered from income taxes until distributed from the fund — and at the same time manage the participation by others in the company.

- One client, as a single-owner firm with fewer than fifty employees, was able to implement a retirement plan strategy that enabled him to increase contributions to qualified retirement plans by close to $500,000, with 93 percent of this going to his benefit.

- A plan my firm developed for two owners of a light manufacturing company with a hundred employees created an opportunity for the owners to make payments into another business, tax deductible to the current entity, and tax-free to the new entity, of up to more than $1 million per year. When they eventually take accumulated assets out of entity two, it will likely be taxed at capital gains rates, rather than ordinary income.

- A family-owned client firm in international sales with forty employees implemented a retirement plan strategy that enabled the owner to accumulate significant liquidity over five short years through the implementation of a pension plan structured to benefit the owner, supporting his planned exit, after transfer of the business to the next generation, with 96 percent of the contributions and assets going to the exiting owner.

Here is another way to describe the power of business ownership. What if you had your own personal retirement *bank*? And because you are the bank's favorite and only customer, let's say you generously promise yourself to double your money every year. If you only deposit $1 and double your account each year and wait for 20 years, do you know what your account balance would be? Over $1 million!

However, the government says you must pay taxes on that growth annually — assume capital gains at 15 percent for the federal government and 8 percent for the state for an overall 23 percent tax erosion.

So instead of doubling your dollar at the end of year one, you now have only $1.77 to double for next year because $.23 went to taxes. That $.23 doesn't sound like much of a loss until you see how much of your doubling is undermined by taxes over 20 years. Instead of more than $1 million, you have a little over $91,000 — more than a 90 percent reduction. And if the government says you must pay income tax rates instead of capital gains, then over 20 years your account will only be $6,400.

We all know the actual tax bill is higher than the above example especially when you add in the ACA tax imposed by Obamacare of 3.8 percent and the higher Federal capital gains tax rate.

The tax code *does* offer business owners the opportunity to grow retirement savings tax-deferred above the limits of typical qualified plans. If you fit the business owner profile specified in the tax code, you can create a substantially larger retirement asset than taxable alternatives.

Use these opportunities to protect against business vulnerabilities and, in turn, increase the value of your business and your legacy.

Takeaways

- If your business is the primary asset in your estate, you are unnecessarily vulnerable.
- Growing non-business assets enhances your negotiation position for Ownership Conversion, and improves financial well-being and future security for your family.
- Federal tax law provides specialized opportunities for business owners to create assets outside the business with favorable taxation.

Chapter 10

The Intersection: Choosing Your Inside/Outside Sale Option

FROM MY experience, most business owners prefer to plan their Ownership Conversion around the insider options. If there are already co-owners, a business transfer may trigger the buy/sell agreement to make Ownership Conversion contractual and automatic.

However, it is an idea common to business owners that the business should stay in the family. The children have grown up with or in the business, and it feels right that they should be part of a tradition if circumstances support the opportunity.

Over the years, entrepreneurial companies can evolve into a second *business* family. Owners want to give the management team and other employees the opportunity to earn ownership and take the firm to the next level.

Each of these insider sale alternatives would appear to reduce the number of variables to control, compared to an outsider sale. However, virtually all the recommendations for controlling the variables I have made remain relevant. What's different is that the *timing* of the Ownership Conversion is not as critical as the right *amount* of time required to prepare and motivate the new generation of family owners without making them impatient.

There's no shortage of negative examples of families and companies torn apart by inside Ownership Conversion. When founders release ownership and legal control to the next generation to enjoy the freedom of retirement, they can still exercise psychic ownership and influential control.

Meanwhile, family members and key employees and partners have their own vision of the future when they are in command and feel pride in their own ways. As promos for TV comedies used to say, *and then the fun begins*. But it isn't fun, except maybe to the attorneys.

Another drawback to inside Ownership Conversions is the fact that entrepreneurs are not noted as patient teachers. Some believe sink-or-swim is the only way to develop self-reliance. Others tend to shield their pupils from the adversity they themselves endured. Either way, most owners have unrealistic expectations of the time it takes to reproduce the knowledge and leadership qualities required for Ownership Conversion.

Remember, *founder* and *successor* are not job descriptions, only relationship labels. Remember also, cloning isn't necessary for insider Ownership Conversion. Different perspectives based on age and experience must be expected and embraced rationally.

Second-generation (G2) owners may not share the entrepreneurial gene, but the genes they got may make them brilliantly opportunistic and great adapters who can lead companies in directions the founders never considered.

Perhaps the biggest obstacle for insider Ownership Conversion is that your key employees, family members, and even co-owners very likely do not have the assets or financial resources to personally purchase the company outright, and may not be bankable enough to attract funding.

To overcome that obstacle, the transaction can be arranged around partial buy-ins that provide ownership and a share of profits for two to three years. With that much time and experience under their belts, they can approach financial institutions with the existing owner to seek financing necessary to finalize a purchase of any remaining shares. This allows the owner to walk away with cash proceeds and without residual risk associated with any long-term installment buyout arrangement.

To summarize the insider sale pathway ...

- Ownership Conversions to co-owners, family members, or a group of current key employees.

- Planning focuses on development, motivation, and retention of owner candidates.

- Timing can be set, but using the duration of time effectively is the challenge.

- The transaction can be staged to provide incremental cash to the owner, and operational cash flow to the insider buyers over a fair time frame.

One of my clients chose the insider sale destination because he believed two key employees were the logical successors for his business. They had been long and loyal members of his company, which made him feel he owed them the opportunity as well. However, we faced a huge impediment to making this a reality — lack of cash. Between them, they did not have the cash or the assets to support such a purchase.

Here are the design components my firm developed for the owner and successors to overcome that obstacle.

- We designed an Ownership Conversion Plan that gave the key employees some ownership in the company and a share of the profits produced by the company each year. This plan included a combination of gifting and sale of ownership interests to take place over a five-year timeframe.

- We also implemented an enhanced PH Personal Hedge for the current owner that allowed him to pull out an additional $800,000 per year on a tax-deductible basis to the business, and exclusively to the benefit of the current owner.

- We put in place the proper documentation to support this plan and created a fully funded contingency plan that would still get the business into the hands of these two key employees if the client developed severe health conditions or died too soon. This design component also ensured the client and his family would receive the full benefit of the business value.

- We then developed a management plan to enhance the growth of the business over the next five years, and gave these two key employees the decision-making input they needed to assume full control of the business at the end of five years and to be reasonably assured that they would be successful going forward.

- At the end of five years, any value of the client's ownership interest that had not been transferred would then be purchased by the two key employees. They successfully secured the financing they needed, because the plan was designed to make them bankable. They had been owners for five years with decision-making input and operational oversight while sharing in profits.

- The whole transaction was designed to get the client and his family to the ownership and financial destination he had chosen. The tax ramifications for the client and the key employee purchasers were reduced by more than 65 percent.

Outsider Sale Planning

Many entrepreneurs decide to take their companies down the outsider sale path and cash out on their terms.

Their co-owners may not be inspired to run the company themselves. Their family members may have well-established careers already. Their management team may feel closer to retirement than ownership.

If your own goals and circumstances fit that profile, and if you apply all the planning recommendations outlined in this book, you can maximize the sale value of your company and position yourself for a favorable negotiated sale. The job is to find the right prospective buyer(s) and work to create an "auction" to maximize value.

Successful firms might receive several calls each year from representatives of potential buyers. Often, the potential buyers are in the same industry looking to achieve scale; some may be direct competitors in your geographic market. If the telephone calls tell you they don't really have a plan and just want to feel you out by tossing numbers in the air, don't get too excited. Even less-inspiring are calls from business brokers who need inventory.

You are different. You do have a plan. Your Ownership Conversion Plan is designed for a *qualified buyer*. That means buyers who know what they want and why they want it. They aren't looking for a colossal bargain. Real value is preferable to undervalue, and the real bargains are companies that are move-in ready.

Having an advisor on your team who deals in corporate mergers and acquisitions and specializes in privately owned businesses can be a tremendous advantage. M&A

isn't always about Wall Street. There are M&A experts and investment bankers focused on entrepreneurial firms in your region and even in your business community. M&A advisors and investment bankers are similar in their offerings, though there are some differences. To some degree, M&A advisors bridge the market gap between transactions that are clearly led by investment bankers (those where the deal size is greater than $150 million) and those led by business brokers (typically less than $2 million). They understand your goals and circumstances and would be excited to represent a company like yours, run by an owner willing to invest several years to create an Ownership Conversion opportunity. They know buyers in diverse industries. They know what investors are looking for and how buyers evaluate companies and their owners. They can help you navigate the equity capital landscape.

Business brokers are another way to go. Business brokers are licensed much like real estate brokers and operate in a similar fashion. Many are well-informed and very capable of discovering qualified buyers and managing the negotiation process. However, like real estate brokers, some are less qualified. You are protected by your advisor team, who can perform due diligence to find the best broker to represent you.

To summarize the outsider sale pathway ...
- Ownership Conversions to a qualified buyer.
- Planning focuses on maximizing value and negotiation leverage.

- Timing depends on economic and market factors.
- The transaction provides immediate cash and minimal risk to the seller.

Imagine selling your company for four times what it is worth today in five short years? One of our clients doesn't need to imagine this because he did it.

His business was valued at $4 million. The Ownership Conversion Plan we designed set a five-year growth goal and implemented strategies to increase the business value to $7 million. By the time we reached the plan horizon, the business was well-positioned for growth and continuity, and it was move-in ready.

Multiple organizations became interested in purchasing the business and the bidding competition raised the company's value to $16 million! That was more than enough to reach the owner's financial destination. In addition to their retirement income bonus, the family could benefit employees and make donations to their charities of choice.

While most of the pre-planning and preparation is the same for both strategies, structuring the financial arrangements for an inside sale and an outside sale can call for totally different approaches. For instance, when selling or transferring your business to family members and/or key employees, we will seek to minimize the value of the transaction for tax purposes and sale purposes. This requires a very different approach, and the more time we have to work on this, the better the outcomes for all parties except the IRS!

Contrast this with the outside third-party sale, where we seek to maximize the value of the transaction. We want the highest price possible to create the highest amount of after-tax cash in your pocket at the end of the transaction. Even with the outside sale, the ability to minimize taxes or defer some taxes while maximizing value is a viable option depending on each owner's unique desires and needs.

Takeaways

- Designed insider sales to family members or management team usually require a substantial investment in development time.

- Insider sales seldom produce an immediate monetization event, and generally utilize a note with incremental cash payments balancing owner and operational cash needs.

- Designed outsider sales can allow owners to cash out and move on with substantial capital for their next ventures or retirement lifestyle.

- After several years creating growth and polishing the company to increase value, outsider sales are still subject to economic and market conditions at the time of sale.

Chapter 11

The Harvest: Reaping Everything Your Efforts Have Achieved

It's not your money! You are just the caretaker of the funds that will eventually go down the government black hole and be lost forever. How does that strike your inner entrepreneur?

Unless you plan in advance and apply the methods available to keep your money, it's perfectly true. True for you and your family and any charities you may be inclined to benefit.

When I have shared this with clients, they look at me as if I have two heads. But then, once I show them the financial realities, they become motivated to take action.

Wealth preservation planning yields many benefits to you as a business owner when your Estate Plan and your business Ownership Conversion Plans are directly coordinated from the beginning. Generally, they are not.

Implementation of the Ownership Conversion Plan typically takes years. Often, owners feel satisfied with whatever estate planning issues have already been addressed, or they look at creating their estate plan further down the road. It's typical to feel overwhelmed and overly satisfied by each separate planning process. Plan integration can seem *optional*.

That's one way to give away control of the family wealth your business success earned. What if I told you it is not impossible for your estate to be depleted by over 50 percent? What could cause that? Federal and State taxes along with estate settlement costs. The black hole.

You can plan consciously or unconsciously. Plan unconsciously and the government will happily plan for you.

Let's say that you are like many of my clients and you are located in the state of Connecticut. We will assume you are in the top income tax bracket for Federal and State purposes, and that your estate exceeds $10.9 million. Assuming you have a spouse, the limit of your gift to your estate is only $5.49 million for 2017.

Here is what happens to each dollar you earn on the unconscious government plan.

- You earn $1 in ordinary income, and you pay at least 49 cents in taxes, leaving you with 51 cents.

- If you were to die the next day, that 51 cents is then taxed at the rate of ~50 percent.

- Your family is left with a net slightly over 25 cents on what began as a dollar.
- 75 percent down the government black hole.
- 25 percent to you and your family!

If, with a few more planning steps to integrate business and estate goals and continuing plan oversight, you could change that allocation to 75 percent for you and your family and 25 percent to the government, wouldn't you want to investigate it?

Why are taxes and the structure of your Ownership Conversion transaction so important? Because without paying very close attention to the impact of taxes on the transaction — whether selling to and outside buyer or an inside buyer — the biggest winner is typically the IRS.

While much of the design of your Ownership Conversion Plan is virtually the same for both inside and outside destinations, the financial arrangements can call for totally different approaches. For instance, if selling to family members and key employees, you should seek to minimize the value of the transaction for tax purposes and sale purposes. Contrast this with the sale to an outside party where you should maximize the value of the transaction to create the highest amount of after-tax cash in your pocket at the end of the transaction.

Sale to Insiders

What are the true costs to buy a business or sell a business? Let's take a look at the cash required to purchase a business for $1 million.

For your insider to purchase your interest for $1 million, they will need to start out with necessary net taxable income from operations of at least $1,755,000, paying Federal taxes at a marginal rate of 43 percent, leaving aside State taxes for simplicity. For you as the current owner, you receive the $1 million and need to pay capital gains taxes at a minimum rate of 23.8 percent Federal. You end up with $762,000 after tax.

So, we start with $1,755,000 as noted above and most of the money goes out in taxes on both ends. The big winner of this transaction is the IRS, as they receive close to 57 percent of this transaction and you end up with 43 percent. If we add in state income taxes, your net and the gross we need to start out with is significantly higher.

Now let's add in what it takes for your business to generate the $1.7 million and look at what you need to produce in gross sales to net the $1 million. Depending on your business structure, the dynamics will be different. However, using a recent client as an example, for the client to pay $1 million to buy out a co-shareholder, he needs to generate $22 million in sales, that's with a 8.5 percent net cash flow and paying the IRS their share.

So as a result of the above, when selling to an insider it behooves you to minimize the value of the business for purchase to the extent you can justify the values and integrate the value with solid and creative Ownership Conversion planning. Then, arrange for most of the cash you need in your pocket to come out to you through various methods that can be deductible by the business, thereby minimizing the cash required to make the purchase and reducing the tax impact on the transaction.

Sale to Outsiders

While it's *their* money, outsiders want to pay as little as possible for your business. As the last section makes clear, with solid and creative Ownership Conversion planning you can raise the value, so that when it's *your* money it's as much as possible.

But even when you succeed on your side, the IRS steps in with capital gains and eventually estate taxes. For tax-avoidance purposes, you need to design opportunities to move value outside of your taxable estate before going to the business market.

If you are charitably inclined, you may have significant opportunities to diminish the impact of taxes on your business sale proceeds, while benefiting charities of your choice as well as ensuring you have income and cash flow for your lifetime. Once you go out to market to sell, it is too late to make strategic moves to minimize the assets that will ultimately be exposed to the tax man. That's one Ownership Conversion design element. There are others.

Every business owner I meet wants to shelter income and assets from the heavy burden of taxation. However, I have yet to meet a business owner who is truly knowledgeable regarding IRS-sanctioned opportunities to accomplish that goal.

Let's assume for a moment that with the help of your professional advisors, you have done everything that you deem practical to reduce exposure to estate taxes within your family and business frameworks. Yet, you still have a current and growing estate tax liability. Depending on the state you live in, it could be as high as 50 percent!

You may have heard of Put Options. As an investor, you may have had occasions to exercise Put Options. Put Options describe a method of transferring risk to third-party financial institutions to minimize or limit your loss on an investment.

You pay these institutions a fee or premium for taking on the risk, which they have deemed is an acceptable one for them. If the event takes place and the value of your equity investment goes below an agreed upon value, the Put Option kicks in and you are made whole by the financial institution.

Well, I adapted that terminology as a "Tax Put" to help clients see a parallel way for them to shift tax risks to a third-party institution. A "Tax Put" makes it possible to reduce the impact on your assets and cash by as much as 90 percent and as little as 50 percent. In turn, you can reduce the cost of paying your eventual tax bill by 50-90 percent.

It's All One Pie So Handle It Accordingly

Whether your Ownership Conversion Plan leads to an outsider sale or an insider sale, it has a significant impact on your estate and legacy planning. Working in a vacuum can be a serious and costly mistake. Lack of coordination and integration can cause personal problems, family problems, business problems, legacy problems, stewardship problems, generational problems, and security problems long into the future.

Your Ownership Conversion Plan began with your vision for your business beyond your tenure. Your estate and legacy planning reflects the same vision. That vision should guide all discussions and planning strategies considered and implemented.

Of course, it is common for entrepreneurial business owners who engage in Ownership Conversion planning to eventually experience planning paralysis. Adding your Estate Plan and Legacy Plan to your to-do list seem easy to defer. You can't. Planning is not an event, it is a process — a perpetual process.

That's where the autonomy, confidence, and conscientiousness that began this book must kick in. Autonomy because only you can claim responsibility for family security and harmony over generations. Confidence because you have the will and the resources for perpetual planning. Conscientiousness because you understand the unintended consequences of decisions made quickly.

If your Ownership Conversion Plan results in a successful outside sale and monetization of your company's value, your planning can focus on wealth management, wealth transfer, and charitable pursuits.

If your Ownership Conversion Plan results in a successful insider sale to non-family buyers, your short-term planning can focus on the conditions of the buyout agreement, followed by wealth management, wealth transfer, and charitable pursuits.

If your Ownership Conversion Plan results in a successful insider sale to family buyers, you need to take steps in advance to integrate your plan with your Estate Plan and eliminate potential conflicts of interest in the future.

In most cases, members of your family who are not involved actively in the business should not be owners. Especially when the family name is on the business, there is a tendency to keep everyone connected to it. Pride is not a good reason for mixing active and passive owners.

Active owners and passive owners have inherent conflicts of interest. One likes to reinvest profits, the other likes the profits to be distributed. Active owners like to make all the decisions. Passive owners want to have a voice in all decisions, even if they are marginally conversant with the issues.

I've seen the tensions grow into arguments and the arguments set off emotional explosions that no one recovers from. It happened in my father's small business. It has happened in multi-generational and multinational business. It has ended with siblings not talking to each other, suing each other, and even doing bodily harm to each other.

Lack of designed planning is to blame. When you plan without design, the IRS has its own very well-designed alternative for you. If you plan without design, in time, family members can and likely will push their own designs forward and create conflict. The problem is too simple to resolve to invite all that grief.

Ownership should remain with family members who are active in the family business. Even then, it is advisable that one active member have a controlling position. You can even everything out with other assets, or use life insurance to equalize asset values. That normally establishes fairness where everybody wins. Add a commitment to transparency and appropriate engagement by the controlling member with the owner and non-owner family members, and you can avoid family conflict.

How you handle the business asset under any Ownership Conversion scenario can also have a direct impact on your personal financial security, the security of your spouse, and the security of your family. It is typically the largest asset you have and requires coordinated planning and action.

Mesh Your Plans

Even though it impacts all facets of your life and your family life and future generations, every part of your plan, and I mean every part, is a reflection on you.

The legacy you wish to leave behind for everyone in your life, including family, employees, and the community at large, can be controlled by you. Estate Plan design components can create proper coordination up front and make the management of all facets of your plan much easier and more seamless.

However, what I see many times is contradiction and inconsistency between the Estate Plan documents and the business Ownership Conversion Plan.

If you want to cause confusion and friction and even cripple your business and shred family feelings, I know how that is done. Unfortunately, so do you. As entrepreneurs, you are likely to do things piecemeal. And once you check it off as done, you probably don't monitor your decisions for changing circumstances and fail to revise when needed.

Ownership Conversion Plans and Estate Plans require consistency and active management. There are many estate planning tools that might seem nominal, but actually could have a significant impact on your business planning. Think about the following examples specifically from a business perspective.

For example, your Estate Plan should include an advance health-care directive that defines your health-care preferences and is to be used only when you can't communicate your wishes. How would that impact your Ownership Conversion Plan if your personal wishes were inconsistent with your leadership role in your business?

A power of attorney for asset management appoints someone you trust to manage your financial affairs on your behalf. The form also indicates in which areas he or she may assist you. If you don't have this form completed and you become incapacitated, a court may appoint someone for you. How would that affect expectations set by the Ownership Conversion Plan.

Wills are used to transfer your assets upon your death. However, even with a will, in most cases your estate will still have to go through the time-consuming and expensive legal process called probate, in which the courts distribute your property. Do you want your business asset and your Ownership Conversion Plan subject to probate?

Living trusts offer another way to transfer property upon your death. They tend to be faster, more flexible, less likely to be contested, and more confidential than a probated will. But from the perspective of your business and your Ownership Conversion Plan, are they properly constructed and consistent with buy-sell agreements?

There are many planning opportunities and strategies that can dramatically reduce the amount of money that goes out in taxes, but they are not DIY (Do It Yourself) projects. Any of them could play a very positive role in the integration of your OCP, estate, and legacy planning.

You have a successful business that has funded a comfortable lifestyle for your family and created personal meaning for you. Now is the time to identify its destination and design the journey to get it there and beyond.

I hope this book has given you insights into the planning process and the impulse to engage in it.

Takeaways

- Insider sales should minimize business value for tax purposes.
- Outsider sales should maximize value for pricing purposes.
- Mixing active and passive owners in your Ownership Conversion Plan is a recipe for conflict.
- Integration of Ownership Conversion, Estate, and Legacy Planning is the key to your wealth management success.

Conclusion

A Future by Chance or A Future by Design?

This is your decision and your decision alone. Will you leave the future of your business and all those that depend on it to chance? OR will you choose Designed Destinations for you, your business and all those who depend on your business?

The investment of time from your perspective can be as little as the equivalent of ONE DAY out of your business life to make a consciously designed and inspired future for you and your business.

I have shared with you some real-life stories of those who left things to chance versus those who chose to design their future.

We have discussed the thinking that needs to go into this process and the key players you should have working by your side to make your consciously designed OCP plan a reality.

We shared the 7 key ingredients of an effective and successful OCP plan. It is my sincere desire that you come away from this very brief overview inspired to act.

If you have any questions on what you have read and desire to have some clarification on anything, you can feel free to reach out to me at the contact information below or to check out our site and blog located at: **www.Designed-Destinations.com**

On the following pages in Chapter 12, I've ended with a Final Exam where YOU will have the opportunity to rate yourself on your level of confidence and awareness necessary to create and implement and effective OCP plan.

Be honest and direct with yourself because you and you alone can dictate the outcomes related to your business. This is your baby, your vision, your process and your choice, a future by chance or a future by design. Let's start that first sentence!

To reach Larry:

lganim@ganimfinancial.com

2429 North Avenue,

Bridgeport, Connecticut, 06604

203-335-0851

Chapter 12

Final Exam

OK DO I have your attention? Would you like to DESIGN your DESTINATIONS? What are the next steps?

How do you rate yourself on the following, on a scale of 1 to 5? A 1 represents you have no idea, and 5 means you have it all locked up!

FUTURE VISION

- ☐ Have you established the date (ex. January 15, 2022) that you wish to stop working in and for your business?
  - Target Date
- ☐ Do you know how much money you may need, annually, after you leave your business to live a comfortable post-business life?
  - After-tax cash flow required

- ☐ Have you chosen your exit path and/or successor?
  - Internal Transfer to Family and/or Key Employees
  - Sale to a Third Party

SIZE OF THE POT

- ☐ Do you know what your business is worth today in cash?
- ☐ Do you have strategies in place to increase your company's current cash flow?
- ☐ Do you know what value you will need from your business to meet your financial objectives?
  - If so, what?
- ☐ Do you know what income your personal financial assets will likely generate beginning on your planned business exit/retirement date?

THE BUTTERFLY

- ☐ Does your company have a business plan *designed* to meet the needs of your plan?
- ☐ Have you assessed and addressed all threats facing your company?
- ☐ Can your key management team run your company in your absence?
- ☐ Does your company have plans in place to ensure key personnel remain committed to the same objectives that you and your company have?
  - Do you have plans in place to incentivize them to stay with the company?

- ☐ Have you done everything legally possible to minimize the taxes you'll pay when you leave your company?

- ☐ Does your company have the systems necessary for a successor owner to operate it successfully?

- ☐ Do you understand and constantly use your company's financial information to improve performance and cash flow?

THE EMPTY CHAIR

- ☐ Do you have a contingency plan in place should something happen to prohibit you from participating in the business temporarily or permanently?

  - Has it been reviewed in the past 12 months?
  - Is it funded?

- ☐ Has your contingency plan been communicated to key players in your business and your family?

THE PERSONAL HEDGE

- ☐ How sure are you that you are taking full and maximum advantage of the unique planning opportunities that you have being the owner of a business to diversify financial assets outside of your business?

- ☐ Do you have a plan in place that will ensure the achievement of your retirement/financial independence objective regardless of what you receive from the sale or transfer of your business?

THE INTERSECTION

- ☐ Do you know which path is optimal for you and your business — selling to an insider, or a third-party sale of your business?

- ☐ How confident are you that the outcome will work for all involved?

- ☐ Do you have a plan to maximize what ends up in your pocket after the sale or transfer?

THE HARVEST

- ☐ Do you have plans in place to minimize what goes out in taxes and maximizes what stays in your pocket and that of your family?

- ☐ Have you reviewed this in the past 12 months?

- ☐ How sure are you that all bases have been covered?

YOUR PLANNING TEAM

- ☐ Are all your advisors truly working as a team or focused only on their individual engagements?

- ☐ Do the advisors working with you have Ownership Conversion experience?

When was the last time the whole team sat at the table together and evaluated planning and strategies in place to achieve your desired outcomes?

About the Author

Larry Ganim's passion for working with the entrepreneur is boundless. He believes that, by helping the business owner, he helps many others as a result. Benefitting the owner also benefits all those who depend on the business to support themselves and their families. A healthy thriving business benefits all.

Larry's passion is evident in every client interaction where honest and direct communication can always be counted on by all involved. His stated life mission—"To be a passionate, loving source of empowerment to others" is fulfilled through his work.

Larry comes from an entrepreneurial family, having worked most of his childhood in his father's business, before entering in his new profession in 1981 when he became licensed as an insurance broker. He began almost immediately reaching out to those he admired most, local business owners learning about their passions and needs. He has focused most of the last 36 years working with the entrepreneur and in 1985 founded his own business around the entrepreneur and meeting their unique needs as business owners.

Larry is the founder and president of Ganim Financial and GFS Wealth Management Advisors, Inc. He has been and is very active in his local community in Connecticut and in his industry, serving in leadership positions on many boards over the years. He is a qualifying and lifetime member of the Million Dollar Round Table, The Court of the Table, and Top of the Table – the highest distinctions in the insurance and financial services industry.

Larry has been honored on multiple occasions as a Five Star Wealth Manager in publications in Connecticut and New York.

He is a father and grandfather and lives with his wife, Diane, in Trumbull, Connecticut.

www.ingramcontent.com/pod-product-compliance
Lightning Source LLC
Chambersburg PA
CBHW020424220526
45464CB00002B/552